Yardwork

OTHER BOOKS BY DANIEL COLEMAN

Beyond "Understanding Canada": Transnational Perspectives on Canadian Literature (co-editor)

Countering Displacements: The Creativity and Resilience of Indigenous and Refugee-ed People (co-editor)

In Bed with the Word: Reading, Spirituality, and Cultural Politics

Masculine Migrations: Reading the Postcolonial Male in "New Canadian" Narratives

ReCalling Early Canada: Reading the Political in Literary and Cultural Production (co-editor)

Retooling the Humanities: The Culture of Research in Canadian Universities (co-editor)

The Scent of Eucalyptus: A Missionary Childhood in Ethiopia

White Civility: The Literary Project of English Canada

Yardwork
A Biography of an Urban Place

Daniel Coleman

Daniel

Sept 2017

James Street North Books is an imprint of Wolsak and Wynn Publishers, Ltd.

Cover image: Michael Gallant
Interior images: Michael Gallant
Cover and interior design: Marijke Friesen
Author's image: Michael Gallant
Typeset in Minion Pro
Printed by Ball Media, Brantford, Canada

The poem on p. 190 is excerpted from *Ojibway Heritage* by Basil H. Johnston. Copyright © 1976 by McClelland & Stewart. Reprinted by permission of McClelland & Stewart, a division of Penguin Random House Canada Limited.

The publisher gratefully acknowledges the support of the Canada Council for the Arts, the Ontario Arts Council and the Canada Book Fund.

James Street North Books
280 James Street North
Hamilton, ON
Canada L8R 2L3

Library and Archives Canada Cataloguing in Publication

Coleman, Daniel, 1961-, author
    Yardwork : a biography of an urban place / Daniel Coleman.

Includes bibliographical references.
ISBN 978-1-928088-28-8 (softcover)

    1. Essays. I. Title.

PS8605.O4435Y27 2017   C814.6   C2017-900982-6

1 2 3 4 5 6 7 8 9 10

TABLE OF CONTENTS

LIST OF ILLUSTRATIONS

Prologue

I LOVE IT WHEN, after the dark of summer sleep, I step out on the back stairs from the sunroom with a cup of coffee in hand and take my first breath of morning air. The early light threads the green leaves of the maple in our neighbour's yard to the east. It filters downward, lighting dewdrops that hang from blades of grass. My eyes narrow when I stretch and yawn, making the prism of dew on a single blade flash emerald, then lime, before winking magenta, sapphire.

The magic of morning in the backyard.

The fire in the dewdrop echoes the flame that leaps when a breeze shivers the scarlet and wine-red leaves of the Bloodgood Japanese maple in the northwest corner of our yard. It is Moses's bush that burns and is never consumed.

I no sooner think, "Take off your shoes – this is holy ground," than a truck, backing into the university maintenance building below our place, flings its backup alarm into the morning air: Beep. Beep. Beep. Okay, maybe not so holy.

The strident noise is cut by a bright, piercing whistle, so sharp and clear it rinses the air of all other sound. It's hard not to smile at the song of a Carolina wren. Its tiny body seems an utterly impossible source for such a huge voice, like a rusted clothesline pulley turned in four or five brisk triplets. Its blazing cycles stop abruptly, leaving the world echoing and ready.

"Good morning!" I answer, trying not to shout, not to draw attention from the maintenance guys below. "Good morning."

How many hours have I spent out here, just like this, tasting the busy silence of an early morning? How many evenings have Wendy and I spent drinking in the sparks of fireflies that hover over the lawn in July? How many afternoons bending our backs to wheelbarrows and rakes, laying flagstone or digging compost? Like every yard in the world, ours is a small plot of earth whose unique personality emerges from both the combination of what's given – the lay of the land, the quality of the soil, the length of the growing year – and yardwork – the amount of care and attention devoted to it.

I'm down to the last sip in my cup. But my heart runneth over.

I am not accustomed to belonging. I am foreign to the idea of staying put. I was born and raised in a spiritual diaspora, and the place in which my family lived was never home. In *The Scent of Eucalyptus: A Missionary Childhood in Ethiopia*, I've described how my parents were Canadian Protestant missionaries who met and married and raised four children in that East African country. The missionary society of which they were part had members around the globe, working originally in West Africa, then spreading across the continent into Europe, South America and eventually Asia. Like the other members of this far-flung community, my parents lived peripatetic lives, assigned by mission administration at different times to different ministries in different places around the country. My mom was born on a farm, so she knew all about yardwork – planting gardens of beans, radishes and beats, as well as zinnias for beauty. But none of the houses we lived in were our own, nor did we expect to stay in them long. The places we lived in, with their unique qualities – from cedarwood floors to painted clay-and-wattle walls – were steps on an eternal pathway, since the kingdom of God was not of this earth and our sights were set on eventually reaching the heavenly Promised Land.

When I completed high school, I followed my older siblings to Canada, the land of our citizenship, which our parents called home, and which we had visited but where we had never lived permanently. I entered university, met and married my wife, Wendy, and eventually graduated from the University of Alberta with a doctoral degree in Canadian Literature. Jobs for literature professors are few and far between, however, so when I was offered a position in my field at McMaster University in Hamilton, we both felt I must accept it. Neither of us wanted to move here. For one thing, our families (the parts that lived on this continent) lived in Saskatchewan and Alberta, and we wished to remain near them. And like most Canadians, we had only seen the glowering smokestacks of Hamilton's steel mills from the QEW's six-lane Skyway Bridge on our way from Toronto to Niagara Falls, and we thought the city looked like an environmental disaster. But there were no other jobs in sight, so we reluctantly moved to this soot-stained, gritty city that grips the southwestern shoreline of Lake Ontario.

Who knows where fondness for a place grows from? Perhaps it is a reaction to placelessness, the un-belonging of my childhood. Perhaps it is part of my increasing perception that in an age of climate change places *have to* matter. Perhaps my growing attachment comes from identifying with this damaged place as an environmental underdog. Certainly, a major turning point in my thinking about this place came from my encounter here in Hamilton with Indigenous thinkers and their understanding that all creation around us is alive and actively trying to teach us. Vanessa Watts, a friend and colleague who is Hodinöhsö:ni' and Anishinaabe, calls this understanding place-thought: the awareness that places are alive, have spirit and are providing us with everything we need to live. I began to wonder if I myself could begin to learn some place-thinking; if I could transfer the skills I had developed in my bookish education toward reading the relationships that constitute a place, a landscape.

But even as I thought about how to get started, I knew immediately that landscape is too big, dense and complex. Anyone who begins to pay attention, real attention, to even one square metre of any place on earth, from the microscopic beings that turn leaf matter into soil to where water goes after soaking into that ground, will soon be overwhelmed. In order for a beginner like me to notice anything at all, I needed to limit my scope. So I decided to focus on my own backyard. I knew that even this small place would be too complex, but at least it would be convenient – right outside my door. I could watch it every day, through each season.

I have become gradually aware, however, that whatever I'd intended, whatever the elements of my upbringing, training and experience that fed my interest in connecting to this place, the place itself rose to meet my interest. Whatever work I have done in this yard – laying stone patios, planting coralbells, digging compost – its own energies, its own particular dynamic of soil and weather and living beings, have responded to and reshaped my efforts. This exact patch of earth in Hamilton, Ontario, Canada, has called me out, responded, seduced, even stalked me. Not to make me into prey – though a growing awareness of its agency, its volition, prickles the hairs on the back of my neck – but to teach me that a feeling of belonging does not reduce the elements of place into belongings, into acquisitions. Paying attention to this place has taught me that belonging is interactive and responsive, not simply assertive.

By relaying what I can about the life that hums in this one place, I don't just pin words on it – it expresses itself, grabs my attention, like the impossible song of the Carolina wren, making me scramble to learn how to hear it. The more I lean in to these everyday voices of this exact place, the more familiar they become, and the more my being and longing come together. I find my longing to know and be known settling into everyday being, everyday life. It's not just that I know more about this place, but that this place increasingly knows me. Belonging comes from having been accepted, not from being in charge. The work of place, the recording of its biography, its life story, then, requires as much listening as it does speaking. Indeed, because of the imbalance of our acquisitive, aggressive times, the work of belonging may require *more* listening than speaking, more contemplation than action, more intuitive immersion than bold assertions.

Ultimately, like all relationships, belonging to a place depends upon good manners: courtesy, respect and gratitude. Good manners are ways of attending not just to the dignity of the lives around us, but also to our need for those lives to remain distinctly separate and not be absorbed into our own, like fuel burned for our benefit. Courteous attention sees the lives that surround us living for themselves, like the maple trees around me that eat carbon and make oxygen. We need them to be themselves, because how will we breathe if they are all transformed into lumber? In this way, yardwork, the labour of attending, has the potential to alert us to what might be sacred in any everyday, familiar spot on this abused, workaday earth.

Holy Land

The earth is sacred. Everything on the earth is sacred. Every spot on earth is sacred, not just certain places that are regarded as sacred sites because something happened there. Something happened all over this earth.

– Audrey Shenandoah (Onondaga, Eel Clan)

THE CAROLINA WREN IS rinsing the air with her song, a truck's alarm is beep-beep-beeping as it backs up in the maintenance yard below our place, and, despite the disturbance, my cup is running over. I am a morning person. I tend to wake up cheerful, so it's not difficult for me to feel joy standing on the back step at this early hour. But I want to do something more in this yard than simply admire its beauty. I want to pay a more focused attention to this exact, little place: to listen, to learn its manners, to register its hidden wonders.

I can't claim any particular expertise. I'm not especially well informed about the environment, though, like many, I'm slowly waking up to the ways in which all things – from the needles on the pine trees to the earthworms under the lawn to the very breath in my lungs – are interdependent and connected. But I know that I need them to stay alive, and they need me. I'm not a scientist or a botanist; I like birds, flowers and bees, but I'm not an expert on any of them. I'm not a historian or a landscape architect. Nonetheless, I want to learn about the layers of story and soil, to be more than just a cheerful visitor who compliments the pleasant views. I want to dig in, to hunker down and figure out where I am. I want to connect with where I've ended up.

Take for instance the cricket that's taken over from the Carolina wren, throwing its vibrating song into the tangy air from somewhere down in the wild ginger we planted beside the stairs. Aren't crickets supposed to make their sounds at night? Maybe this one is late to bed. And why doesn't his song ever pause? I watched a YouTube video showing how crickets make their sound by rasping one wing over the barbs on the other, like running a thumb across the teeth of a comb. Their upraised wings form membranes that amplify the chirp. The YouTube crickets had wings only half an inch long that created a rhythmic pause while they flipped the wing back down to the bottom to start the upward rasp. *Chirr. Chirr. Chirr.* But this cricket in the ginger never pauses. Why? How does he make this continuous, unbroken sound? Maybe he's faster than most. Maybe he whips that wing from the end to the beginning so fast I don't hear a pause.

I have no idea.

It's just male crickets who sing, by the way. They have a whole songbook from which to sing: a loud song to catch a female's attention, a quiet one for courting them when they come close, a sharp one to warn off other males and another to celebrate the joy of union. Entomologists call crickets' rasping action *stridulation*, and they say there's a relationship between the rate of stridulation and temperature. Crickets are cold-blooded, like all insects, so they stridulate faster when it's warm and slower when the antifreeze gets thick in their veins. An American scientist named Amos Dolbear in 1897 came up with a way to tell the temperature from cricket chirps. He counted the number of chirps a snowy tree cricket made in fourteen seconds and added forty to that number to come up with the temperature in Fahrenheit. This formula is known as Dolbear's Law.

My cricket doesn't seem to have heard of Dolbear's Law. The morning is plenty warm, twenty-five degrees, and it's only seven a.m. The cricket's song is non-stop. I can't count Dolbear units, because all I hear is one unending chirp. Maybe crickets here in the city of Hamilton don't stridulate like snowy tree crickets did for Dolbear.

That's the thing about the livingness of things: by paying attention, by learning the manners of a place, you can learn a whole lot. Enough even to make a law. But then shift locations, listen to a different story, pay attention to a different cricket in a different backyard in a different place, and nature changes the rules.

But you have to notice in the first place to even begin to wonder. Here in this city, the traffic's either too loud or I'm too busy to stop and notice minor details. The world goes on right beside me every day. Mornings like this one, however, make me want to stop and take note. They make me want to fend off my ever-present busyness, dampen the outside noise and focus in. They call me to do some yardwork.

SO WHY NOT START at the beginning? With this morning's first light sparking the fire in the maple, it's easy to think of first things. Beginnings, however, are difficult. Where exactly should a person start? "In the beginning God created the heavens and the earth," from the book of Genesis? The universe started with a big bang? And what existed before the beginning? Most stories posit a murky and shapeless dark before the quickening of light and life. "And the earth was without form, and void," says the Bible, "darkness was upon the face of the deep. And the Spirit of God moved upon the face of the waters." Without form and void – that's a way of saying that whatever existed at the start, we just don't know. It's we who are in the dark.

Here in this morning light, dewdrops tremble on blades of grass, within earshot of transport trucks groaning up the highway to the top of the escarpment that curves around the city. In the rumble of nearby traffic, anyone might find it hard to imagine that dark and formless time, to picture how things were then. The even grade of the neighbourhood's sidewalks, the level lawns around each house on this street, the web of utility, TV and fibre-optic lines – none of these conjure up formlessness and void. None of these link us to a time when only dark water rippled below, only black sky spread above and in between, just wind – the living, breathing air. No ground, no trees, no sun or moon. Genesis insists that the Spirit of God – some kind of sentience, some kind of presence – hovered over the waters. So the void wasn't exactly void, but our language for what animated the scene is vague and abstract.

The story of beginnings told closer to here is more concrete, has more detail. This is the story told by the Six Nations, the People Who Build the Longhouse – which is what their name, Hodinöhsö:ni', means. Their story of beginnings says the Guardian of the Tree with Lights in It, Hodä:he', had woken from a dark dream saying the people should uproot the tree under his care. After carrying out these strange instructions, Hodä:he' and his wife, Atsi'tsiaká:ion, sat eating a ceremonial meal at the rim of the hole in the Sky Dome, where the roots had been unearthed.

I'm afraid of heights and don't like to think about their legs dangling out over the null and void below, ocean or lake smell wafting up from the absolute black beneath their heels.

Another version has Atsi'tsiaká:ion sending her husband to scrape bark shavings from the briny roots of the sacred tree. She was pregnant, and the tree had power in it – so much power that it glowed. Everyone knew the tree was sacred, something not to be touched. Hodä:he' was nervous and slow. But Atsi'tsiaká:ion was heavy with child; she wanted medicine and didn't have patience for a hesitant husband, so she brushed him aside, stepped to the edge and . . . slipped. Some of the longhouse people say she fell through the hole in the sky by accident; others say that Hodä:he' pushed her. Maybe he was angry with her for telling him to disregard taboo and touch the sacred tree. Maybe her supercharged hormones blinded her to how close she was to the edge of the hole.

It's not for us to comment on the behaviour of sky people.

So the woman fell, and as she did, she grabbed desperately for a handhold. All she could grasp was a fistful of little plants and roots, not enough to hold her. Some waterfowl, floating on the black water below, saw the falling woman and decided to fly up and ease her landing.

So, according to this story, the world was not really null and void at the beginning. There's a backstory before the Beginning, a kind of prequel that has bird and animal nations living on earth's water before the sky people arrived. This beginning before the beginning only mentions water creatures – no crickets. Perhaps that's because there wasn't any land yet, no place where the non-stop crickets of Hamilton could stridulate.

The waterfowl conferred, as they carried the falling woman on their wings, about where they could put her down. Some flew down and held council with the animals living in the water below. What to do? Finally, A'nó:wara the turtle, the most solid and dependable of all, volunteered to let the woman land on the hard shell of her back. Atsi'tsiaká:ion was thankful for the firm place to settle, but she looked around and saw it was hard and bare. She showed her new neighbours the plants and roots she had grabbed as she fell and explained that she needed to plant them in soil. She needed a yard to live in, a place to tend her few roots and seeds, strawberries and medicines, if she was going to survive.

The humblest of all the creatures, Hano'gyeh Muskrat, volunteered to dive to the bottom of the deep and bring up some earth for Atsi'tsiaká:ion to plant her fistful of baby plants. Different layers of the story tell this part differently: some say that other beings, such as Beaver and Otter, dove down first, and that the water was so deep they came up empty handed. Empty pawed. Some versions even say they died in the attempt. Another version has Hano'gyeh diving alone and being down there for a long time, while everybody waited anxiously. It is said that his body finally floated, lifeless, to the surface. Beaver looked closer, though, and was surprised to find mud clutched in his paws. This mud from the sea floor dried on Turtle's back, the brine of lake weed evaporated and Muskrat's mud smelled more and more like earth. Atsi'tsiaká:ion danced in circles of gratitude, and as she did, the soil spread out like pie dough until it covered all of Turtle Island.

She danced out the place where I now live, including this yard, where I stand today.

MUCH OF WHAT I just said is full of loaded words and mixed up names. I've hardly begun to tell the earliest story from this area, and already I've stumbled into controversial territory. The longhouse of the Hodinöhsö:ni' people is made up of a series of rafters or nations. Officially, there are six of them, each with its own language: Mohawk, Oneida, Onondaga, Cayuga, Seneca and Tuscarora – although others, such as small groups of Delawares, Tutelos and Nanticokes, also adhere to the longhouse. The names I'm using are a mix of longhouse languages. The name Atsi'tsiaká:ion comes from Mohawk, while Hodä:he' comes from Onondaga. Hano'gyeh is an Onondaga spelling for muskrat, while it's spelled Anò:kien in Mohawk. Say them both out loud and you'll hear the echo. Different names and spellings indicate where different versions of the story originate. I've used the version of Atsi'tsiaká:ion's name from the Mohawk storyteller Sakokweniónkwas, also known as Tom Porter, who learned it from his grandmother, among others. And I've used the version of the husband's name from a long line of tellers and retellers. Sotsisowah, also known as John Mohawk, a Seneca professor at the University of Buffalo, updated a transcript of the story originally written down by the Tuscarora scholar J.N.B. Hewitt, who worked at the Smithsonian in Washington, DC. Around 1889, Hewitt came to the Six Nations of the Grand River – today just a half hour's drive south of here – and heard the story from elder and Onondaga chief John Arthur Gibson.

Given these inter-linguistic, inter-national sources, it's understandable that the names I'm using might get confusing.

Professor Mohawk, now deceased, was not Mohawk but Seneca. He re-edited the story from a transcript made by a Tuscarora ethnographer, who heard it from an Onondaga chief. The point is that it's an old story that's been passed from tongue to tongue, language to language, generation to generation, reserve to museum to university and back. It's as layered as the limestone cliffs of the Niagara Escarpment that outline this end of the lake. At least all these tellers have something in common: all are members of the longhouse builders of the Iroquoian Confederacy.

But there's a history of bad blood in the name Iroquois. The Mohawk writer and language teacher Brian Maracle says the French may have heard the name Iroquois four hundred years ago from the Algonquians, who were rivals of the Hodinöhsö:ni' and called them "Irinakhoiw," meaning "real snakes" or "rattlesnakes." The Algonquian Confederacy rivalled the Iroquoian one for trade, and their epithet would have pleased the French, who disliked those "snakes" for preferring to deal with the Dutch and the British. So they spread the word.

But I just called Maracle a Mohawk, another Algonquian insult meaning "cannibal." The Mohawks' name for themselves is actually Kanien'kehá:ka, which means "people of the flinty ground," after the rocky terrain in eastern New York, along the waterway known today as the Mohawk River. But they've had so many years swimming in English, whether they wanted to or not, that the old language has mostly been washed out. I've heard Hodinöhsö:ni' people use the old curses to name themselves today, often with a chuckle and a shrug.

These names grow out of ground that is contested and shifting. I have cobbled them together from books by Hodinöhsö:ni' people who speak different languages, from outsiders, from the internet and from the beginner's class in Mohawk language I took a few years ago. I offer you fair warning: take my words with a grain of salt, because they are as mixed up as the sand and cobble of the ridge upon which this yard is built.

Even putting the story of Atsi'tsiaká:ion and Hodä:he' at the front of this book raises problems, because creation stories are sacred to the people who hold them. Over the years, these sacred Hodinöhsö:ni' stories have been raided by anthropologists and museum collectors who don't practice the everyday duties and ceremonies of the people to whom they belong. They don't wake in the morning to utter the Words That Come Before All Else, known as the Thanksgiving Address, which recognizes the order of Creation that welcomed Sky Woman into a world that provided everything we humans need. They don't perform the Four Sacred Ceremonies that re-enact the agreements between people and the more-than-human world that keep nature's cycles turning. Those of us foreign to these practices don't know what it means to bring these stories to life in our everyday world. Treating them as legends, myths or academic curiosities kills their vitality, like taking a butterfly fluttering in the coralbells here in the yard and pinning it to a board in a glass box. Not something you want to do with Sky Woman.

I'm caught, therefore, because a settler society like ours is built on both erasing and glass-boxing the stories of the people who were here before us. Without an active awareness of First Peoples and their stories, it's easier to think of our ocean-crossing founders as peaceful settlers and to ignore the culture killing that was part and parcel of land theft. If we act like there aren't any stories of those who lived here before our ancestors arrived, we take over without memory or conscience.

The longhouse stories grew out of this land, out of this part of northeastern America. Out of this territory of Great Lakes, limestone cliffs and Carolinian forests. They were passed on by generations of people who had watched and listened to this particular habitat for thousands of years. Well, not *exactly* this habitat, at least not any more, since ninety percent of what's growing here in my yard – the Japanese maples, the Russian sage, the hybrid tea roses – are imports and hybrids from Europe, Africa and Asia. Our ideas of flower gardens, lawns and city streets have changed this place dramatically. But all around and underneath these newcomers, the foundation of the ancient habitat remains. And longhouse stories help us attend to that ongoing, living foundation on which everything else – all the new imports – depends. These stories reconnect us to the laws and agreements by which the natural system works. "The primary law of Indian government is the spiritual law," writes Syracuse University professor and Onondaga Faithkeeper Oren Lyons:

> It has been the mandate of our people to look after the welfare of the land and its life. Central to this responsibility is the recognition and respect for the equality of all of the elements of life on this land.... If all life is considered equal, then we are no more or no less than anything else. Therefore, all life must be respected. Whether it is a tree, a deer, a fish, or a bird, it must be respected because it is equal. We believe it is equal because we are spiritual people. (5–6)

From what I've learned so far from Hodinöhsö:ni' people, stories such as Atsi'tsiaká:ion's fall from the sky function as ceremonial narratives that dramatize nature's laws of equality and interdependence. They teach us about the agreements upon which all life depends. These stories are what Mi'kmaq scholar Marie Battiste and Choctaw legal philosopher Sákéj Henderson call the "cumulative result of a large number of historical contracts, which create reciprocal obligations of kinship and solidarity among all the species and forces which co-exist in that place" (45).

This is a very different idea of story from those I'm familiar with – from Goldilocks and the Three Bears to Adam and Eve in the Garden of Eden. More than this, I'm new to these parts. My ancestors and I haven't lived here long enough to accumulate thousands of years' worth of historical contracts, or to understand the reciprocal obligations that make our ecosystem work. In attempting to keep track of these stories, I'll for sure miss things that are important, and I'm bound to twist their meanings with my newcomer's accent and way of thinking. But by passing on the fragments I've learned, even if my understanding is partial at best, at least I won't be spreading the lie that this storied place was null and void before Europeans arrived.

LIKE THE HODINÖHSÖ:NI' PEOPLE, geologists say that in the beginning there was water, and that the land rose up from it. They also say that animals walked the earth long before people. Scientists mark the passage of time through the stories they find in rocks. In the layers of limestone, dolomite and grey shale in

the escarpment walls, they see that this place, including my backyard, was once a warm, tropical sea.

When the hostas in my garden are buried in three feet of
snow in January, it's hard to think tropical, to smell the jacarandas
or the coconut oil. But even I can read the evidence told by the
escarpment that surrounds us. Seashells, water creatures and
coral petrified in layers of stone travel downwards through time,
all the way from the Longwood Formation near the top crust
through at least six layers to the Grimsby Formation below.

There is a scaffold of galvanized steel stairs and platforms,
protected by railings, on the north side of the Dundas Valley, near
Rock Chapel Road. There, geologists from the Royal Botanical
Gardens have bolted signs onto the cliff face that introduce walk-
ers to the stories the layers tell. Walking down those stairs is like
stepping down the bleachers of nature's great amphitheatre. The
top tier is the most recent. It consists of glacial till: clay, sand,
gravel and pieces of fist-sized cobble held in a tangle of tree roots.
The grip of these roots, however, is unpredictable, and the rubble
of shale and stones at the bottom of the cliff indicates how readily
they can let go. The signs call the second tier under the till the Lockport Formation. It drops five or six metres, and is subdivided into
two beds: the Ancaster Member and the Gasport Member. The difference between the two is clear, even to a novice like me, because
the Ancaster layer consists of brick-shaped chunks of sand-grey
stone, while the Gasport layer is a single smooth wall. The signs
indicate that the Ancaster is thinly bedded dolostone made from
sediment laid down when the warm and shallow tropical seas were
calm, while the Gasport is thick-bedded and coarser grained, laid
when Hano'gyeh and the others were enduring choppy waters.

Although the signs don't mention muskrats or turtles, the Gasport layer provides the first traces of the water plants and animals that existed here before sky people or humans. The smoother surface of this section of rock, not as creased and cracked as the Ancaster Member, reveals the contours of sea lily crinoids and cavities called vugs that were once the tunnels of sea worms.

It is just as the Six Nations story says. In the dark beginning, before this place was formed, already things lived. The evidence of their living here remains in the rocks. Theirs is an even older beginning than stone itself.

Geologists say the rocks indicate that a warm, river-fed sea covered what are now Lakes Huron and Michigan. The rivers flowing into this sea laid down silt, layer on layer – some clay, some sand, some the crushed shells of sea creatures and coral. They say that about four hundred million years ago, the basin of that sea began to rise up, not unlike Anó:wara rising from the deep. The edge of the draining sea lifted into what's now the cliff face of the Niagara Escarpment. In the drying that followed, not to mention the glaciers of four distinct ice ages, they believe erosion carved from the dry sea floor the cliffs and slopes that now define this region.

My footsteps ring out from the metal stairs, echoing off the cliff face as I descend from the Lockport Formation to the Rochester Formation, made from the chalk of mollusc shells. Then comes the dolostone of the Irondequoit and the brick-sized chunks of the Reynales Formation, which remind me of the Gasport and Ancaster Members above, before I encounter more sandstone and shale the next tier down, in the Thorold Formation. In the delicate wafers of this shale, I feel like I'm closer to the moment when the sediment was laid down in the first place. The piece I lift flakes in my fingers. It smells cool, like basement dust. The story of time unfolds from tier to tier, sometimes repeating itself, but never in the same order. Finally, at the bottom of the cliff, I reach the crumbled talus slopes that mostly cover the Grimsby Formation. The signs say there are more formations below the Grimbsy, but I have to take this on faith as they are completely covered by fallen rubble that leans against the bottom of the cliff.

The story registered in the stone tiers of this great amphitheatre suggests another reason for the dark beginning. After the warm seas, it got so cold that this whole region was capped in ice – a thick, hard, frozen shell between the light of the sky world and the formless void of water and muck below. The deep freeze lasted for ages, and left some remarkable traces. Bones of mammoths were unearthed in the 1830s, when the Desjardins Canal was dug through the Iroquois Bar, the massive ridge of gravel that divides Cootes Paradise from Hamilton Harbour. Today it's known to most people as Burlington Heights. When the leaves have fallen in winter, you can see, from the top of these galvanized stairs, how the High Level Bridge spans the old cut of the canal.

The geologists say the ice cap in this area began to melt twelve to fourteen thousand years ago. As the ice thawed, a lake, larger than present-day Lake Ontario, formed in the bowl bounded by the Niagara Escarpment. Eventually, the ice dam that had contained this huge lake collapsed, and meltwater rushed out the eastern end. Scientists call the body of water that rushed from this area "Lake Iroquois" – not to be confused with the warm tropical sea from back at the beginning. They named it after the crude French epithet for the Hodinöhsö:ni', despite the fact that the Hodinöhsö:ni' stories I've heard don't talk about a drained lake. That's what I mean about finding stories that don't line up exactly, even though they have echoes.

Lake Ontario is what we have come to call the smaller body of water we live beside, the lake these cliffs shore up, the child of massive Lake Iroquois. In the Mohawk language, "Kaniatarí:io" means "nice or beautiful lake." Some sources indicate there were similar words in Huron-Wendat, so perhaps we got "Ontario," too, from the mixing of languages. However we got the name, and despite its smaller size, the longhouse people must have thought the lake enchanting to give it such a name.

So, this land rose up on Turtle's back. Or the tropical sea sank away. However it happened, what had been dark and formless surfaced and revealed the escarpment that embraces this end of the lake. Forces and powers – call them trilobites or Tree of Lights, ice dams or muskrats – lived and breathed in the darkness that existed before anything we know. Something hovered over the deep and built this amphitheatre before any humans filed in to occupy its bleachers.

THESE STORIES ARE NEW to me, since I arrived here only twenty years ago. Like many people, I moved here for a job. So I didn't learn the stories about this place at my mother's knee. And she didn't hear them from her grandparents, or they from theirs – which means that I've had to seek out these local stories. I've read them in books, talked to people who have lived here longer, gone hiking in the valley and on the escarpment, walked the trails, tracked the creeks, headed on down to the museum, checked the library and browsed Wikipedia.

I'm like many who have moved to the sprawling cities that hunker down more or less like permanent work camps around this end of the beautiful lake. Johnny-come-latelies, we wonder where we are and what we have to do to survive in this place.

Or we don't wonder at all. We remember all too clearly why we came here. Terrified by armed men knocking on the door back home, shrunken by nothing to eat, or assaulted by cholera or a terrifying tsunami, Hamilton's immigrant generations boarded a diseased and dirty ship or breathed the greasy air of a red-eyed overseas flight. For many compelling reasons, those of us whose story is about moving want to leave our hardship in the past and strike out into a fresh, untroubled world.

We are the people-who-move, migrants and the children of migrants. We move heaven and earth, not to mention ourselves. With hard work and know-how, we move everything: falling water into electric light, dark forests into waving wheat, previous residents onto reserves, swampy shorelines into terra firma for factories, docks and piers.

Move and improve.

And, if the place doesn't improve fast enough, or won't keep pace with our drive, we move again. If the apple farm gets blight or the sky turns yellow from our smelter's dust, then we light out for new territory. We get used to moving, which makes us fidgety, to say the least, about staying here, staying anywhere. We arrive and absolutely love a place. But it's not long before we run our shit into the creek, and the creek flows into the bay, and the bay is where we get our drinking water. All it takes is one generation before there's an outbreak of cholera, and the city fathers have to fill in a mass grave. A hundred and fifty years later, we can't believe it when a veteran tugboat captain runs aground on a pile of toxic waste by one of the factories' piers in Hamilton Harbour. The pattern doesn't seem to change over the generations. Once the shit surfaces, we sell our erstwhile dream home to someone else. Maybe some Irish family fleeing famine, or African Americans fleeing slavery, who then sell it to Italians or Portuguese after the war, who then sell it to Vietnamese or Serbians or Somalis after other wars. There is always someone fleeing violence or poverty that got here even later than we did. We hope they haven't heard about the cholera or cancer in the bay.

What are the chances of those-who-move becoming people-who-stay, becoming folks who give up the fidgety dream of the Promised Land somewhere over the rainbow and begin to think of here as precious, even sacred – as holy land?

I was raised on Bible stories. My childhood was soaked in tales from what we called the Holy Land, the place where all the episodes in the Bible took place. From the Jewish beginnings, with the null and void, the garden and the apple, the exile and forty years of desert trekking and onwards to the extermination of the locals, the settling into the Promised Land and another exile in Babylon. Then comes the Christian part, with its storytelling throughout the towns of Galilee. All of this, including Jesus' death and resurrection, the stories of the twelve apostles and the early spread of the Church, fed my childhood, shaping my spirit and imagination.

We called the land in the Bible holy because its layers of stories, stacked one on top of the next, added up to the Book of God. The Holy Land is where *it* happened. Where everything happened. Where God touched down and lived among people. Literally, we understood it to be the land God had given people after their many tribulations.

This biblical story of exile, of seeking the Promised Land, permeates popular culture, even when its source has been long forgotten. "Next year in Jerusalem," Jewish families repeat every Passover, the ritual phrase heavy with the grief of exile and the longing for an elusive home. Christians have reworked this idea into allegory. Rather than a literal story about wandering in a desert, they understand that it's about finding a way through this vale of tears, not to Jerusalem but to a heavenly city, where they can finally put down their troubles and rest. The idea of progress – that through science, democracy or technology, we are gradually bettering our conditions and creating a better future – is beholden to this moving and improving, as is Manifest Destiny – the idea that the pilgrims who arrived in America were, like the Chosen People, leaving oppression behind and building a new city on a hill, where justice, liberty and Walmart would prevail. This story becomes a historical cycle. "Exodus, movement of Jah people," sang Bob Marley, syncopating the story of white colonial migration with a call for black people to rise up and throw off the Babylon that Manifest Destiny had grown into. The biblical stories have created a kind of unconscious language, a spirit map, of where we came from and, ultimately, where we're headed as nations, societies, revolutionaries and aggrieved people seeking justice.

I confess: I love the Bible. I'm not outside its mental geography. This book has shaped my mind as much as anybody's. I know it's been used for some vicious purposes, but so have other good books, from the *Mahabharata* or *The Communist Manifesto* to *The Catcher in the Rye.* The same book can be used to justify slavery and abolition, justice and apartheid.

But what does representing a territory in the Middle East as the Holy Land make *this* land, right here under my yard, beside this lake, beneath these limestone cliffs? Does it have to remain Babylon?

For those still building the longhouse with its six rafters, some of whom have a huge affection for the Bible, *this* is the Holy Land. This is where *it* happened. This is where the beginning began, where the stories start. This Holy Land is where ancestors descended from the torn sky above, where they avoided drowning in the dark waters and landed safely on Turtle's back, where everything we need to live a good life was first provided. This Holy Land is inscribed with the features and creatures of this exact place, this northeastern piece of Turtle Island, the shores of this beautiful lake, these cliffs and pine-guarded woods. This is *it.*

SOME TAKES ON THE Bible story need rethinking. When I was a child, we used to sing the Jim Reeves song in my boarding school's chapel:

This world is not my home, I'm just a-passin' through
My treasures are laid up somewhere beyond the blue.
The angels beckon me from heaven's open door,
And I can't feel at home in this world anymore.

What I did not know, as a boy in chapel, is that, like a lot of American pop music, Reeves's song had its antecedents in the experiences of people who had been kidnapped into slavery. Only when I got older did I learn that they'd been stuffed in the holds of ships like so many sacks of sugar or barrels of salted cod. That they had been stolen across the ocean. Many did not complete the journey. Some jumped overboard. Those who survived were driven by axe handles, musket butts and whips, like so many animals. How could such a brutal world feel like home?

It's no wonder slaves sang of passing through and seeking treasures beyond the blue. Some of them arrived here in Hamilton, after months on the Underground Railroad. Stewart Memorial Church on John Street is famous for being one of the stops. So is Griffin House, west of here, in the Dundas Valley.

This is a part of the story we didn't know when we belted out the tune in chapel. But even then, some of us knew that there were families that beat their own children, countries that ate their own citizens; that sometimes you have to flee a bad scene if you want to survive, let alone grow. We liked the song for saying that we could let go, that we could be free. We liked knowing that we were made for life beyond the blue; that we didn't have to grab on tight to bitterness, as if it were our only option. We could seek other worlds, other places, beyond this one, where we might be better off.

But here's the part that troubles me: What happens to the place itself, if every generation is just a-passin' through? If every generation chops down the trees, exterminates the Canaanites, clears a farm, then a strip mall, dumps chemicals in the water and moves on? As the number of people on this earth passes seven billion, what are the chances of finding a Promised Land to move to that hasn't already been promised and settled, abused and compromised, where living residents, human and non-human, aren't already being beat up or disappeared?

THERE IS ANOTHER STORY from the Bible that I think holds more promise. It, too, is about how things started. But instead of starting with the formlessness and void, it starts with words: In the beginning was the Word. It's a kind of puzzle that has kept generations of readers guessing. I can't be sure, but maybe it means something like, everything started with Talk. According to this version of the creation story, the world starts out with or in word. It's as if the word was Creator and the Creator was word.

Rather than starting with darkness and void, with zero and *terra nullius*, this story starts with expression, with talk. It begins with intention and expression, living and humming with Hano'gyeh and the others before the Beginning. I'm inclined to think this version suggests that a place becomes maples and wrens and crickets and rocks and trees and escarpments through story. Or, to put it the other way around, that maples and wrens and crickets and rocks and trees and escarpments *are* the words with which the place and its stories begin. I'm inclined to think that without telling, without these living beings speaking their existence, Creation would have remained null and void, dark and out of focus. Once words start, then everything – every single thing – emerges. Creation is expressive. Expressiveness is creation.

Seen this way, expressiveness is the basic power, the ultimate energy. It's what makes things happen.

Scholars of semiotics, the science of signs, have a term for this beginning. They call it *logocentric* – *logos* in Greek means word, so word-centred or word-obsessed. They hear the statement "In the beginning was the Word," and they say, "But have you noticed that the word is unsteady?" Words are slippery. They are not as solid as the things they refer to. They lean on each other like dominoes, and if you trip one, then the whole string collapses.

What else would you expect of bookish types? They are smart, but nerdy, too. *Of course* words are unstable. Every time I try to string a sentence together, I know it. I feel it every time I know the thing I was trying to say has eluded me and the words that came to mind missed the mark. Every time I feel trapped by something I said yesterday. It sounded all right then, but it's come back to bite me, because I didn't know how my words would land in someone else's ear. Of course words are unsteady.

But that's just one side of it. The other side is this: there's no way to get around words. Pretty much all the things we know – and a whole lot of things we don't – start with words. They begin with talk and story, and are made into solid objects or marks on a page. They are stored away in clay jars or libraries or memory sticks so that we can go back and check on them, or carry them with us wherever we go. *Here's the earliest record,* we say. *See how our story began?*

But even those words, the ones in the jar or in the library, seem to shape-shift each time we dig them out again. If they always meant the same thing, we would not need the shelves upon shelves of books, written over the centuries, that suggest new ways of understanding the same, original words. Have you ever seen one of those huge volumes of the Torah in a synagogue? All those footnotes about what Rabbi X in 1738 said the original text meant, and how Rabbi Y in 1834 disputed X's view until Rabbi Z changed it all around again? Sometimes there are more footnotes and addenda than original words! Of course words are unsteady, or you could say mobile, even when they look as frozen as the Gasport Member.

But it's not just the Bible that suggests we start with talk and story and word. Not just people who take their constant marching and moving orders from the book. Because, for one thing, other beings talk, too. Don't forget Hano'gyeh and the other water people, let alone those vociferous rocks.

I'm sitting and writing in one of the outdoor chairs on the patio under the white pines, my feet up on a cushioned footstool. As I scratch out these lines on the page, a glossy black squirrel ghosts slowly under my chair, a walnut, husked of its green casing, clenched in his mouth. Maybe that's why he was so unusually unhurried and self-effacing. He didn't want anyone else to see his prize.

Except me. I'm an exception. Not competition, in the world of squirrels, for the pearl of great price, which he carries silently and boldly under my chair. He noses this way and that. Reading the signs of other beings' passing, of the places where this particular walnut might find safe storage. He slips soundlessly under the leaves of the Francee hosta, searching for a place to bury his treasure.

The leaves where he vanished haven't stopped shivering when the sky overhead fills with the shriek of blue jays calling their own names: Jay! Jay! Jay! Jay! Four siblings who have been rolling around our neighbourhood all summer like kids on skateboards swoop into the white pines on the west side of our neighbour's yard. Their adolescent guffaws overwhelm a sound I had not been aware of until it stopped. The intimate chitter of a mother Carolina wren, hopping to its fluttering baby in the lower rungs of the cedar hedge. I saw them earlier, silhouetted in the thin branches at the north end of the hedge, black against the green wall of leaves in the neighbour's yard. The young one crouched excitedly, fluttering its stubby wings, while the mother inserted her beak into the baby's greedy mouth. Chit, said the mother, hopping back one twig. Chit. Then she was off for another seed or bug.

I am aware that each of these beings expresses itself all day long in my backyard. Just because I don't know their language doesn't mean they are not speaking, not making words. It's like being in a circle of people speaking a language I don't know. I get used to not trying to understand. I can recognize the rise and fall of intensity, of what I imagine might be sounds of distress, laughter or straightforward information, but it washes over me like water washes over fish. It doesn't enter my consciousness.

This is how our culture has become deaf to Creation's words, to the self-expressiveness of many forms of life. We have decided that humans are the only ones who speak. So we don't hear what any stridulating insect, any reeling Carolina wren, any slab of dolostone, is saying. It's a kind of focus that becomes a bias, a refusal of a holistic understanding of words and communication. The root of "whole" is the same as the root for "hale," meaning healthy, which is the same as the root for "holy." You could say our deafness to more-than-human words is how the land became unholy, unhale, unwhole.

But whether we listen or not, it'll go on talking. Nature doesn't mind repeating itself.

Since I'm not from here, but want to *belong* here – to be here a long time, in a healthy place – I will do some yardwork. I'm keen to try and track as many stories as I can: the ones that started here, like the maples down the slope, and the ones that landed here more recently, like the Japanese painted ferns beside these stairs. All of them keep speaking their existence, right here. And because words are slippery, because each one leans on its neighbours, tracking the stories of this place means I can't grip one so tightly that it squeezes out the next. Maybe this is what ecology means; maybe it means attending to a whole and holy ecosystem of stories. Instead of listening to just one word or just one story, maybe tuning in to all the stories that jostle together in any given place, maybe this messy process will help me, help us, understand the piled up layers – the cracks and seams that run through them, their interdependencies – that distinguish the "thisness" of this place. Maybe gathering up these broken stories will help those of us who moved here begin to feel something. For the place. Itself.

This Actual Ground

Even now that has become old which you established – the Great League [of Peace]. You have it as a pillow under your heads in the ground where you are lying.
– "Traditional History of the Confederacy: At the Wood's Edge"

SO, WHAT ABOUT THIS exact place? The dirt and rocks and grass and concrete that hold me up when I walk around right here in this yard?

When I think about the ground, the picture in my mind is of complete darkness, because the ground we walk upon is something we can't really see. Of course, I see the surfaces – the grass I stand upon here in my yard, or the parts that rise up in the air, such as the amphitheatre of the escarpment. Under the surface, however, is mostly beyond our notice. We rely every day on the confidence that its unseen layers are absolutely here. But most of us know very little about what's under that surface, invisible to our eyes. While it's possible to put a glass window down into the earth, as people do when they watch ants make their rooms and tunnels, what the glass shows is not really earth going about its own business. It's more like a biologist's diagram: how roots extend their fibres down into the soil, where white grubs feed upon them. A glass cannot reveal the mysteries of the dark we all depend upon.

The Creator twin, De'hae'yawa:kho', grandson of Atsi'tsiaká:ion, said that the earth is always doing two things at once: it's thriving with life, and it's also always dying. When he made the first humans and animals, from whom we all descend, it is said that De'hae'yawa:kho' took some of that earth that Hano'gyeh had brought to Anó:wara's back and shaped it into the bodies of all the living, moving beings. He then breathed into their lungs, and the creatures came to life. But because they were made of earth, they would all eventually die and become earth again.

The Creator in the Bible did a very similar thing: took earth and breathed into it to form Adam, whose name comes from the Hebrew "adamah," meaning "soil, dirt." That's where the biblical saying comes from: "Ashes to ashes, dust to dust." The ground is a rotating cycle that looks, at first glance, as if it has gone still, the wheel no longer turning. But regardless of what we may think, it's moving, all the time. We know this, but we also don't know it. Or it doesn't really register. If we think about it too much, it makes us dizzy – the same way it's hard to walk if we think the ground is moving and might not be there to support our next footfall.

But sometimes we're given reminders of the ceaseless life underground, like the mystery that happened right here, twice, in this backyard, and still has me scratching my head.

I emerged one morning and paused on the back step to enjoy the light spring air. The sun was shining, and after being cooped up indoors through the winter months, I was relishing the freedom of being outside without a coat or mitts, breathing in the scent of cherry blossoms and new leaves. I was about to limber up for the day with my morning push-ups when I noticed one of the mottled grey and white stones in the patio tipped like a sinking ship, its backend saying goodbye to the heavens and the prow diving to the depths below.

I built this patio myself five years ago, after we'd finished the addition on the back of our house. I'd done my homework and had decided to dry-lay it. This meant I did not pour cement between the stones but set them in screenings from a quarry. Dry-lay avoids the inevitable cracks that occur in concrete when the ground shifts. It's amazing how much ground is jostled about by frost, moisture, even drought. And when the ground moves, heaving the stones, I can just lift and resettle them. With all the quarries in the region hauling builders' stone, landscaping boulders and flagstone, plus gravel, out of the escarpment, it's not hard to get a truckload of screenings, which is the fine stone grit and powder that falls through the finest screens or sieves in the gravel yard. In other regions, people lay the stones into sand, but screenings are spongier than sand, and, because they have so much lime in them, they congeal around the stones once everything's been set in place. My version of stone-laying went like this: I dug out the rectangle of the patio to a depth of nine inches using a pick and shovel. The digging and wheelbarrowing gave me a sore back at first, but after a few days I loosened up and my back felt even better than before I started – unkinked and strong.

Luckily, the soil behind our place is more loam and sand than clay. As I dug, I tried to make the cool subsurface slope gradually away from the house so that when I was done, the patio wouldn't flood water into the basement. Then I rented a packer, which looks something like a gas-fed lawnmower but with the motor bolted onto a hefty flat plate instead of a whirling blade. The rotation on this machine is offset, so when I cranked it up, the whole unit jumped and jiggled and bucked like some kind of rodeo beast. I grabbed on to the handle and rattled my bones round and round the exposed soil, which that heavy plate pounded hard and flat as a sidewalk. Then I added three-quarter-inch-sized gravel to a depth of six inches. Once again, I brought out the rattling, gasoline-belching beast, which pounded that gravel until it, too, was a sidewalk.

By this time, I felt a hum all through my arms, shoulders, back and down to my legs – even after I shut off the rodeo. Later that night, after a beer, a shower and something for supper, I could still feel my kneecaps twitching – like those road construction guys must feel after breaking up asphalt with a jackhammer. Next day, once I got my muscles unwound enough to stand up and walk, I wheeled in three inches of sand-coloured screenings. I spread them evenly with the edge of a long two-by-four. As I did so, I kept checking the level to make sure the whole surface continued to slope away from the house.

Now I was ready to lay the stones. First, I got a bucket of screenings, a small hand shovel, a hammer and some scrap pieces of board. I spread out a layer of soft screenings and settled the first stone into it. Niagara Escarpment flagstone is undulated, never perfectly flat or even. Its shape reflects its beginnings in the tropical sea, in sediment laid down in ripples. The quarries make these flags by splitting them along fault lines formed aeons ago in the ancient sea. These lines are fairly even, but not machine even, and the stones would rock if I didn't snuggle the dips and hollows of their undersides into the spongy screenings. I learned to pack the screenings in around the edges of the stone by tapping on the end of a scrap of one-by-two board with a hammer – similar to knocking in a tent peg, except the scrap is blunt, not sharp, so it packs the screenings rather than digging a hole. I would tap in some screenings, add a handful or two more and keep packing it tight around the edges of the stone. I found the scrap of wood around the edge worked better than a rubber mallet on the stone itself. If I hit the stone too hard or in the wrong place, even with rubber, it would break where I didn't expect.

The job was repetitious: a layer of screenings, then another mottled, rippled slab of stone, tap all around until it didn't wobble when I stepped on it. Then the next, and the next, until I had covered the whole area. I was using random rather than square-cut flags, so the entire patio was like a puzzle never meant to fit together. The stones were heavy as I lifted each one into place, and I could feel the repeated crouching in my knees. I could only do two or three hours of work a day. The cool, dry smell of limestone screenings permeated everything: my hair, my gloves, my boots and my pants pockets. It took about six weeks to build the biggest section of patio where this one piece of flagstone, five years later, is diving into the ground.

So, after all that packing and gravel and screenings and tapping, how did this stone get tipped up like this?

I walk out to the upended stone, slip on some heavy leather gloves and use a pry bar to shift it off its spot and onto the others around it. Staring up at me from the stone's bed is a six-inch hole, black and round as the pupil of an eye, right there in the screenings I had pounded flat five years before. I get down on one knee and have a closer look. I call into the hole, in case some animal is down there.

No reply.

Gingerly, I put my gloved hand into the cool, sandy dark.

Still nothing.

The hole drops eight inches or so, and then makes a ninety-degree turn toward the lawn, only a few feet away.

What could have made this hole? Water? Animal? An old tree root, now decayed? It looks the same size and shape as the groundhog hole I found in the strip of Carolinian woods between our place and the maintenance building down the hill. But here? I read somewhere that groundhogs sometimes dig their tunnels as far as forty feet, so I pace it out to the little shin-high fence at the back of our place. Mrs. Forbes had strung this fence along the top of the ravine to keep out invaders like groundhogs back when this house was built in the 1940s. She was a fierce gardener who hated the ceaseless cropping and chewing of critters.

Eighteen to twenty feet. I guess it's possible.

If this is a groundhog tunnel, however, it's a spectacular failure, trying to surface where there's a ceiling of stone. And there is no sign of an alternative exit anywhere else in the yard.

I ask my neighbour Mark if there was ever a tree here back in Mrs. Forbes's day. He thinks there was an evergreen, maybe a spruce or fir, but not right here. It had been closer to the corner of the house. I guess a tree root could reach this far, but if this hole is from a decayed tree root, why didn't I see rotting wood when I was digging out the patio and pounding in the gravel?

A hole tunnelled by water doesn't seem a likely cause, either. Rain once washed down some of the screenings over near the addition, where the earth was still settling after the construction crew dug out the basement. That figures. There would have been soft soil eight or ten feet down, so a heavy rain could have sluiced mud down into cavities left by the backhoe. It is amazing how much soil can be carted away by underground water. There's a spot down at the street corner where the sewer under the asphalt connects to the one under Sanders Boulevard. There must be a fault in this connection because every few years, city workers have to dig up the thin crust of asphalt around a hole that keeps reopening in the tarmac. Underneath is a hollow crater where the running sewer waters have leeched away yards and yards of roadway substrate. This is a fairly common phenomenon in sewers built under roads. One of the crew members working on our street drains told me that an entire tractor-trailer truck once fell through the surface on Burlington Street and into one of these underground sinkholes caused by gravel-eating storm sewers. He said most people don't realize how often we are skating over thin asphalt covering a subterranean void.

But I don't think this is a sinkhole caused by water. Escaping water wouldn't make a perfectly round hole like this. The flagstones that sank near the addition wall formed a basin where the screenings slumped down into the ground and not a pristine, vertical tube.

I don't want to dig up the lawn trying to track where the tunnel goes after it elbows eight inches down in the screenings. It would be too much work, for one thing, and I'd have to reseed the grass after. So I shrug my shoulders, buy ten bags of screenings, lift the surrounding grey and white flagstones and start over again. I don't rent a packer this time, since it's only an area of four or five square feet. I pound the new screenings into the hole with a heavy iron pipe that has a six-inch round metal plate on one end. I smash them into the hole as hard as I can, then spread a new bed of screenings, mash it down with the tamping pole and tap in the flags with my piece of wood. It's a hot, sweaty Saturday's work, and once I've swept the finishing screenings between the stones, all I have to show for my effort is what I had originally: a flat patio surface.

Which is why it is particularly exasperating to see, the next year, the same area starting to sink again. Frustrated, I find the old pry bar standing with the rakes and shovels in the garage and use it again to lift the flagstones. This time, there is no perfectly round hole below, but a more general depression. I'm guessing that water is the culprit this time, seeping down into the parts of the hole I couldn't reach with the tamper last year and taking some of my screenings with it. I try to think of other causes, but none occur to me. So, once again, I'm tamping more gravel and screenings with the iron pole, laying down the heavy flagstones, tapping around their edges with the one-by-two and sweeping the last screenings between the flags.

I'm glad I went with dry lay, since the whole thing is still a mystery. The earth is alive, and it's always dying. Twice now I've wrestled with an unknown cycle occurring in the ground, out of sight until it causes trouble on the surface. Who knows when I'll struggle again with this unseen force busy in the dark underside?

THEY SAY THAT PEOPLE who know themselves are *grounded* – that is to say, they are solid, don't fly from who they are. They're comfortable in their skins even though they're made of dust, of earth. They know all youth and beauty will one day wrinkle. They aren't deluded about the everyday stuff they're made of, and knowing these things doesn't cause them to panic. They accept that the mutability of everything made from earth is just another fact of life. So they root themselves in the real, in the everyday soil. My friend Barbara once said that spirituality is about building a relationship with reality, not about living in a world of illusions that has nothing to do with the ground you live on. Many people have ideas about what makes them spiritual, and a good number of these are pie-in-the-sky ideas like heaven, paradise, nirvana or, in the words of the song we used to sing, "This world is not my home. I'm just a-passin' through."

Rather than aiming skywards, the Hodinöhsö:ni' – like my friend Barbara – look down. They say the principles of the Great Law of Peace on which their longhouse confederacy depends lie in the ground, like a pillow under our heads. For them, peace isn't projected into the ethereal future. It's here and now, arising from the very land on which we live. There's a certain kind of energy – for me, a sense of actually being alive in a place – that comes from knowing I'm made of everyday dirt and no bull about it, from building a relationship with this reality. Investigating the hole under my patio reminds me that the earth is alive, is crawling, even booming, with life. It's full of bacteria and micro-organisms and roots – full of the everyday mystery and dynamism that keeps everything alive. I can't see into the ground, even though everything I do rests on it. This fact requires trust. If you don't trust the ground on which you live, you will never think of it as a pillow where you can take your rest.

And here's the goosebumps-on-the-back-of-the-neck part: the nutrients, the life force in the ground, come from impermanence, from death and decay. This land is holy because it literally contains the lives of our ancestors: grandparents, food plants, animals, microscopic enzymes and nutrients. Every plot of ground is a sacred burial site on which our lives depend. As Onondaga Clan Mother Audrey Shenandoah said, "Every spot on earth is sacred, not just certain places that are regarded as sacred sites because something happened there. Something happened all over this earth." It doesn't matter where you are, what's dying in the ground feeds what's living in the ground. This reality seriously ramps up the admonition to attend to and respect the ground on which we live.

Consider, for example, the black plastic kitchen composter on the east side of the house. When I turn the pile inside it, wine-coloured worms wriggle and twist away from the light. Silver fish flee to the shadows. Fruit flies storm up in a cloud from black banana peels, from blue powder crusting mouldy bread, from browning orange peels and soggy coffee filters. The stench causes my nostrils to clench, and the shovel slurps when I jerk it up out of the mess of scraps. That bin of compost lets you see and smell what happens in every animal's guts – how bright red strawberries, white daisies, the three sisters of corns, beans and squash, sweet-smelling whole wheat bread, shiny green pea pods sag into shit, a stinking, writhing slop falling into pus and stench.

I comparison-shopped compost bins online when buying ours. The folks on one website call it tea, that diarrhea that oozes from this mess – compost tea. As if it's their toddler's potty-training treasure. And it is a treasure, if you think about it. There's no growing, no greening, no leaping, leaf-uncurling new growth without this nutritious tea.

In fact, you could say that the ground itself is a massive compost bin. It takes everything that falls into it and mushes it up in its dark, warm intestines, to make the soil for whatever grows next. The ground under our feet is the compost of who and what has lived here. It is also the power and energy of everything alive and breathing. We are the standing-up-and-walking-around part of the cycle. Our reality grows from the lives decaying and feeding this living, breathing world. When I think of it this way, I realize there's a lot of relating to the reality of this place – to any place – that we haven't yet done.

I'm like anybody else and would rather avoid the pus and stench of life, the simple paradox of trusting in the dirt.

This backyard, for instance, the flat piece of ground I call our garden, spreads north from the house thirty feet or so to a short retaining wall of concrete blocks before spilling into the ravine below. How much of the dirt of this yard was put here on Turtle's back by Hano'gyeh? How much sits exactly where the glaciers left it as they scraped through the Dundas Valley, when Lake Iroquois was becoming Lake Ontario? How much was shaped and scraped by human hands?

The soil in this garden seems too good to be true. When I was planting the Bloodgood Japanese maple that our friend Brent gave us as a housewarming gift seventeen years ago, I dug down three feet to make room for the root ball. The ground was so soft and loose I never had to stomp on the shovel blade. The steel found only mealy, sweet-smelling topsoil all the way down. Not like the rock-hard clay along the side of our house and toward the street, where shrapnel exploded from each chop of my pickaxe when I was digging the gravel bed for our new sidewalks. The dust chuffed up by the pickaxe smelled dry, like powder. Nor does this topsoil have the light colour of the sand in it that the backhoe clawed out of the ground ten feet down when they were digging the basement for the addition. The backhoe's pile was like the sedimentary layers of the Rock Chapel cliff face, but in miniature and in reverse order: light brown sand on top, layers of sand and clay in the middle, black topsoil at the bottom.

I ordered seventeen yards of topsoil from a garden centre when we first moved into this place. Think about that for a minute: the power and vitality of all those lives lived in another place, even if only down the road, brought here in the back of a truck and leavened into the lives of this land here. A friend and I bent our backs and wheelbarrowed the truckload to all the perimeter gardens. Seventeen yards raised these gardens by only two or so inches, nowhere near the three feet I dug down for the root ball. I wonder if Mrs. Forbes (nee Clarkson) and her mother and sister did the same thing back when they built the place – did they bring in truckloads of black loam and spread it along this ridge over the legacy of sand and gravel from long-ago glaciers? Or maybe the Forbeses had nothing to do with it. Perhaps this rich soil is from the geologists' story, with its centuries of sediment from the bed of that warm tropical sea. And there are other layers, too. I wonder if this soil was composted more recently from forest leaf matter, before the woods here on the edge of Ancaster Creek, were cleared for crops by the Binkley family who arrived in 1800 and whose multiple generations farmed the area for about one hundred and fifty years.

Our yard pushes farther back into the ravine than anyone else's along our street. Our neighbours tell us Mrs. Forbes was famous for her gardens. She won awards for them from the 1950s through to the 1980s, when she was in her seventies. We bought the house from the Morrisons, who bought it from her. They told us about her, but she was ninety-one and dying the summer we moved in. We never had the chance to meet her, let alone talk gardening. I would love to see photographs of her gardens, but none of the neighbours I've talked to seem to have kept any. I've looked at our house's blueprints from McDonnell & Lenz Architects, Hamilton, dated June 1948. They show concrete footings and weeping tiles, but don't say what was to be done with the earth dug out for the basement or how far back the yard should go.

In the end, any effort to build a relationship with the reality of this exact place has to be interested in its layers, both known and unknown. I don't know what kind of mix we're living on – how much recent invention, how much an ancient place? There are the parts of its biography that we do see – the green lawn on the surface – and there are the parts we don't see, like mysterious, six-inch-round tunnels bumping up one day into the solid canopy of a flagstone patio.

The ground may be a pillow on which we lay our heads, but we only dream its life beyond the reach of direct and confident observation.

SOMETIMES, IF YOU'RE AT a public event where speeches are being given, you will hear the person at the mic say they want to acknowledge the people whose traditional lands we're standing on today. That's if they think of it. Many times, they don't. But if they do, they'll acknowledge "the Hodinöhsö:ni' people" or "the Anishinaabe people."

Around here, this too is tricky.

If you know local history, it's not exactly clear whom you should acknowledge. How far back should you go? All the way to the falling woman Atsi'tsiaká:ion and Hano'gyeh the muskrat? I've read archaeological articles that call the first human groups to live at the head of Lake Ontario the "Princess Point Complex." It's a strange-sounding name that makes me think of either a psychologist's diagnosis or a gated community in the suburbs.

Archaeologists have dug up broken pottery, arrowheads and traces of corn at several places around southern Ontario, including right here at Princess Point and Bull's Point. That's why they call it a complex – because there are bits and pieces here and there, and they don't know if they are all evidence of the same people or not.

Princess Point and Bull's Point thrust into the Dundas Marsh a couple of kilometres from here. I often take the canoe down there and paddle around the shallow dish of muddy water and cattails known as Cootes Paradise. This marsh is where Spencer, Chedoke and Borer Creeks flatten out across the valley floor on their way to Lake Ontario beyond the Iroquois Bar.

Every one of these names tells you something, even as it hides something else. I've already talked about the word "Iroquois." And then we have this whole mix of British family names tumbled up with the names of English and Scottish towns – Spencer, Dundas, Burlington – where early settlers originated. Princess Point adds its own strangeness. It was only in the imaginations of Europeans that Indigenous people in this region had kings and queens, let alone princesses. So the name adds an element of fairy tale – a Pocahontas-style story brought to you by Walt Disney.

You could say that's what all these English names do, in a way: they paste a European fantasy over whatever was here, whatever the actual people living here said about the place. More often than not, the new name has stuck so well that we don't know anymore how people used to think about or understand it. A name like Princess Point *creates* a prehistoric null and void.

But for those who dig a little deeper, it is possible to read the remains of corn and pottery. The scientific scrutinizers of ancient people's trash piles aren't certain whether these Princess Point people were Algonquian hunter-gatherers or Iroquoian agri-culturalists, and whether they had lived here for centuries or if Iroquois-speakers migrated in and pushed out the Algonquians. They know these people were some of the earliest corn growers in the northeast of Turtle Island and likely had inhabited this region by 600–750 AD. Archaeologists base their belief on what they've dug up from ancient firepits, where people burned corn cobs for fuel. Fire preserves pieces of these cobs that would oth-erwise have turned into compost, allowing today's scientists to carbon date them.

Sites are also dated by determining whether discovered fragments of pottery were made using coil or paddle-and-anvil techniques. I am guessing this distinction separates ancient pot-ters who coiled a snake of clay round and round to build the walls of a container from those who used a paddle to build up the sides, like mudding plaster on a wall. By comparing corn and pottery remains here with those found in places such as Pennsyl-vania, scientists try to determine if the Princess Point Complex evolved here, or if there was a period of dramatic migration – say, when corn growers displaced hunters and gatherers, or when coilers gave way to paddlers. At this point, they're not sure. So, if we are going to acknowledge the first people to live around here, the earliest we know about are those that lived on the little peninsula we now call Princess Point.

Later still, archaeologists say other Iroquoian and Algonquian peoples came and went through this area. The names we have from this period are Huron, Petun, Neutral and Erie. Scientists have found signs of how these groups of people lived in this area dating back to around 1300 AD. They know the people at that time lived in longhouses, cultivated corn, beans, squash and other plants such as tobacco and sunflowers. They used pottery, tobacco pipes, baskets and many kinds of stone tools. Through reading these kinds of evidence and checking these findings against what was recorded by the earliest Europeans to arrive in the area, historians say an Iroquoian-speaking people called the Attawandaron lived right here at the Head-of-the-Lake. That's the tribal group I've heard most often named as the "original" inhabitants of this region.

But their originality derives from their being the first people referred to by the earliest European travellers to document their impressions of this area: the Frenchman René-Robert Cavelier, Sieur de La Salle; the Sulpician missionary René de Bréhant de Galinée and his companion François Dollier de Casson; and the Canadian-born traveller Louis Jolliet. These four met up here at the Head-of-the-Lake in September 1669 and stopped at an Attawandaron town they called Tinawatawa, on a portage path that would have followed one of the creeks up from the lake as far as canoes could go before scrambling up the escarpment to join the old Mohawk Trail on top. Eventually, it would lead across the uplands to the Grand River, and from there, either downstream to Lake Erie or upstream toward Lake Huron.

Historians have not been able to determine exactly where Tinawatawa was located. That portage route could have bridged off from Ancaster Creek, in the valley below this backyard, for all we know. The town would have been somewhere above the escarpment, as the lake edge and marsh down below in those days was dense with marsh reeds, razor grass and mosquitos, not to mention hard-to-navigate bog. People came down to the marshlands for lake rice, salmon, berries and waterfowl, but they tended to build their villages on top, where it was easier to get around and not so buggy. They would have lived near water, causing some to wonder if the place the four explorers called Tinawatawa was near what's now the hamlet of Mineral Springs. There they would have lived in the shelter of Carolinian forest, but near open prairie lands that would have made it easier to grow the three sisters.

Once the British and French newcomers arrived in the northeastern part of North America in the 1600s looking for animal furs and gold, the Hurons and Iroquois got pulled into the Europeans' trade rivalries. It was not long before the Huron-Wendat confederacy had lined up with the French and the Hodinöhsö:ni' with the British in a decade-long series of raids and retaliations known as the Beaver Wars. Between 1640 and 1650, the two sides traded furs not just for iron kettles and pots but also for iron-headed tomahawks and muskets, which increased their lethal capacity.

As the violence between the Hurons and Iroquois escalated, pressure grew for the Attawandaron to choose a side.

They tried not to, which was why La Salle and the other visitors called them "*la Nation neutre*," a name that hides as much as it shows. The more authentic-sounding Attawandaron also hides and shows, because it's a Huron name, meaning "people whose speech is a little different." Basically, people with an accent – like the Algonquians calling the Hodinöhsö:ni' "snakes," and the Kanien'kaha:ka "cannibals."

The Neutrals or Attawandaron tried to run this area as what was known as a Dish With One Spoon, a kind of commons where enemies could collect food in peace. As it is today, the lake then was a major transportation route, and this end of it was full of fish and waterfowl. Cootes Paradise held a bounty of wild rice, berries, more fish and yet more waterfowl. Even today, the marsh where I paddle my canoe maintains the greatest concentration of animal and plant species of any area of similar size in all of Canada. As many as half the fish living in the western end of Lake Ontario hatch in Cootes. So back in the day, this place was a high traffic supermarket, and it worked in everybody's favour if nobody brought a knife or a spear to chase off others. But with the wars over beaver pelts and guns intensifying, this delicate balance became too hard to maintain. Violence escalated and the Hodinöhsö:ni' first decimated the Attawandaron, and eventually the Hurons, too. Many believe the Hurons were exterminated during these wars, but the Iroquoian tradition of adopting survivors means that some who now live under the Six Rafters have Huronian ancestry. The military victory in the Beaver Wars allowed the Hodinöhsö:ni' to expand their trade and hunting territory north of the lakes from their original home in what's now upstate New York.

But as I learned with the tipped-up patio stone, the ground is never still. All the packing down and hammering in the world doesn't settle things forever. Likewise, the Iroquois didn't have free run of this region for long, even after the Beaver Wars, because once the Hurons and Attawandaron lost their hold on the area, an even larger nation of people from the west, the Anishinaabe, pushed into the territory through what's now Ontario.

By the 1700s, the Anishinaabe (also known as Ojibways or Chippewas) had established control over most of the territory north of Lake Ontario, and a subgroup of them called the Michi Saagiig were regulars around the Head-of-the-Lake, especially at the mouth of the Credit River. Their presence in the region explains why the British, when they needed to solidify their administration north of the Great Lakes – after being pushed out of the thirteen colonies during the Revolutionary War – made a series of deals with the closest native people in the area, the Michi Saagiig Anishinaabe, to buy sections of what's now southern Ontario. Eventually, they bought Toronto and what's now Mississauga – which is an English approximation for Michi Saagiig. But first they bought this area in 1784 – basically the whole Niagara Peninsula – so they could legalize the squatters who were already building and farming in the Niagara area. What they needed most urgently was land on which to settle their military allies, the Six Nations.

So when someone wants to recognize the traditional territory we're standing on, which original people should be acknowledged? The Princess Point Complex? The Attawandaron? The Michi Saagiig Anishinaabe? The Grand River Iroquois? Each of these is partly right and partly not. Our house and this whole city

are built upon living ground, and the lives composting within it
are many layered, complex and interwoven.

THE PEOPLE WHOSE NAMES do get acknowledged on street signs
in my neighbourhood are the Binkleys. We're on Binkley Crescent, and around the corner is Binkley Road. There's a Binkley
United Church on Main Street, two blocks from here, and there
used to be a Binkley School – now called Binkley Hall, renovated
into apartments for university students. The Binkley name is posted
all over this end of Hamilton, because Marks (1747–1805) and
Mathelena (1751–1838) Binkley's purchase of approximately eight
hundred acres occurred when the grid-work of European names
and streets and maps were being superimposed onto this region.

A person has to think about this for a minute. This place
has been bustling for thousands of years. Deer, Carolina wrens,
red oaks, hummingbirds, Princess Point people, white pines,
turtles, glaciers, Attawandaron, Michi Saagiig, muskrats and
Hodinöhsö:ni' people have passed through, inhabited, fought
over, rooted, made homes or nests, settled seeds into every crease
and corner. But it's not until someone fences off a piece and registers it as private property that a human name gets stuck on the
place. There's a big difference between calling a place the Dish
With One Spoon, or even the Head-of-the-Lake, and calling it
Binkley Crescent.

It's a very different relationship to reality.

The Binkley family's names are etched on the headstones
in the little cemetery back of our place, just fifty metres to the
west of our yard. Marks (sometimes spelled Marx or Marcus)

and Mathelena (sometimes Magdalena) are buried there. They were known as Palatine Germans, or Pennsylvania Dutch, a corruption of Pennsylvania Deutsch, referring to the low German language spoken by seventeenth- and eighteenth-century refugees from religious wars in southwestern Germany and Switzerland. Many of the Pennsylvania Dutch were known as nonconformists, because they had dissenting beliefs for their time – truly, for any time. These nonconformists didn't believe in killing or taking oaths, and they believed in adult rather than infant baptism. Today, most of these groups are known by the names of their distinct sects: Mennonites, Amish, various kinds of Anabaptists. Their beliefs brought them repeated trouble in Europe. They would go to prison and endure torture rather than pick up a sword to defend or dethrone one of Europe's bishops, kings or queens. In 1683, in an effort to escape religious or aristocratic violence, a large group of them arranged with William Penn to move to his colony in America.

When I read on Marks's moss-green tombstone that he was born in Lancaster County, Pennsylvania, I assumed, along with several local histories I'd come across in the library, that the Binkley ancestors were part of that Mennonite story.

I was wrong. History is never as straightforward as it looks.

The local histories I'd read presented the Binkleys as leading members of the entourage of Pennsylvanians who founded European settlement in the Hamilton region – families including the Hornings, Hesses, Rymals, Filmans, Bowmans and Lyons. But these written accounts were inconsistent and sketchy, and I wondered if there was a surviving family member who might help me dig past the surface of the Binkley story. Surely a family once so prominent in this region would have a descendant with a more detailed knowledge of their history.

It took me about a year and a half to follow the trail, but an inquiry at Binkley United Church put me in touch with their archivist, who took some months to dig through old notes to find an email address for a descendant now living in England. After several email exchanges spread over another half year, this individual put me in touch with Carol (Kennedy) Binkley and Mary Ellen McDonald McBain, whose mother had been a Binkley. Carol and Mary turned out to be the kind of passionate, detailed, thorough family genealogists I had been hoping to meet.

My email inquiry sparked a ready invitation from Carol to meet her and Mary at her home just twenty minutes' drive from me in West Flamborough. The three of us gathered on a sunny winter afternoon in Carol's dining room, around cups of tea and a plate of cheese and crackers. Carol and Mary hefted onto the table binder after heavy binder containing pages and pages of clear page protectors brimming with meticulously filed notes, family trees, newspaper clippings, cemetery records, photocopies from history books and photographs. Voices bright with energy, they explained that the two most common mistakes about the Binkley family are that they were: one, Mennonites, or two, United Empire Loyalists.

"They were neither," said Carol, a retired schoolteacher who knows a good story depends on thorough homework. "The Binkley ancestors in Switzerland were Reformers, Lutherans who disputed some of Luther's doctrines. During and after the Thirty Years War, that part of Switzerland was divided into cantons ruled either by Reformers or Catholics. Both sides persecuted the nonconformists. So, as Reformers from the Canton of Bern, the

Binkleys would not have been friends of the Mennonites. Even so, the religious wars during that time displaced people of all religious stripes, and Marks Binkley's father, Hans Michael Binkley, migrated to Philadelphia on the *Billander Oliver* in 1735."

"Yes, and they weren't Loyalists either," added Mary, handing me a page from the red binder in front of her. She seemed quieter than Carol at first, but the spark in her eyes flashed a gentle inner fire. "You see, Hans Michael's oldest son, Johann Marks Binkley, who migrated from Pennsylvania and bought the original farm where you live, had served as a captain in the *American* – not British – army during the Revolutionary War. So they weren't pacifists, and they weren't Loyalists, either."

"And," Carol beamed cheerfully over her glasses, "Marks is recorded on the Pennsylvania tax rolls in 1782 as a tavern keeper, so they also weren't teetotallers. According to the autobiography of a man named – let me see here – Christian Ritter that is kept in the Pennsylvania State archives, George Washington and his retinue stopped at Binckley's Inn – spelled with a *c* – on the morning of October 2, 1794."

I'm thrilled and relieved to have met Mary and Carol. They have saved me from reproducing common mistakes. I had written an earlier version of this chapter, in which I described the Binkleys as Mennonites who were part of the chain of migrations that took place at the turn of the nineteenth century from Pennsylvania to St. Jacobs in Waterloo County, north and west of Hamilton. Carol and Mary helped me correct my account. From our lively tea-time conversation – and from the four huge binders they generously loaded into my car – I learned that the Binkleys were indeed part of that Mennonite migration, but that they were not Mennonites;

that the Binkleys were indeed part of the wave of Loyalists who fled post–Revolutionary War America, but that they were not Loyalists; and that the Binkleys were not the original owners of this exact plot of land, nor was their name exactly Binkley.

Reading through the binders, I saw seven different spellings of their name, including Binggelli, Binkele, Pinchelie, Pingley, Pinckley, Binckley and finally Binkley. Carol said she knows there are Binkleys up in Hanover, Ontario, who spell it Binkle without the *y*. These all appear to be different spellings for a similar pronunciation, because she once met a Swiss gentleman who explained that even the Italian-looking Binggelli would have been pronounced pretty much the same way. It appears that the name Binkley settled into its Anglicized form only after the family established themselves here in Wentworth County.

The Marks Binkleys arrived in 1800 from Lancaster County, Pennsylvania having passed through the Allegheny Mountains and crossed the Niagara River at the sandbar known as Black Rock Crossing, after which their party followed the Niagara Escarpment, stopping at the farm of Abraham Horning, a countryman from Lancaster County who had arrived the year before. The Binkley entourage had left in early spring and didn't arrive here until mid-June. Apparently, they had done well in the tavern business, as they carried silver money with them, and travelled with cattle and considerable goods in large, unwieldy wagons that required them to chop down trees and widen the trail along the way. They arrived, weary and footsore, at the home of their friends the Hornings, grateful to rest for some days in the barn. Next they would be taking on the heavy labour of breaking the trail for their wagons through the Beverly Swamp northwest of here on their way to Waterloo County, where Pennsylvania neighbours had said there was good, cheap land.

Local historian T. Roy Woodhouse writes that the Binkleys and their party gathered at the Hornings' farm on the escarpment brow with the Filmans, Lampmans and Bowmans on their first Sunday here for a morning service of thanks and praise for their safe journey. Marks, apparently, had the "gift of the tongue," while Peter Bowman had "found the light" – so much so that the open-air service lasted three hours. This was followed by a feast of pigeons, fish, potatoes and sour bread, accompanied by hemlock tea sweetened with maple sugar. Details like these provide a tantalizing glimpse into what ingredients and provisions would have been available for newly arrived families at the Head-of-the-Lake in the 1790s. Livestock were too precious to slaughter because of the milk and eggs they provided, thus the wild meats. Similarly, true tea from India was too rare in these parts even for settlers with means, so local plants sufficed, as did sweetener made from local maples. Spirits and stomachs satiated, the celebrants took a walk to the escarpment edge where the vista opened onto the Dish With One Spoon below, extending from Lake Ontario in the east, across Cootes Paradise directly ahead and to the Dundas Valley rolling out to the west. Marks and Mathelena were entranced by what they saw.

"Marks," she murmured. He was lost in the splendour before him and didn't respond.

"Marks," she said again, more loudly and determinedly. He reluctantly disengaged his attention from the lake and valley below to see what she wanted. "Marks, dear," Woodhouse reports her as saying. "We will seek no further. This shall be our home."

"That's how they ended up in Hamilton," Carol said, pointing me to her copy of the Woodhouse chapter. It's clear she loves this story, as do others who have tracked the Binkley family story. It gets retold several times in these binders.

I love the story, too. It wasn't mere real estate that drew them here. Yes, the land was verdant, and they could see in it good potential for farming. But it was the beauty of the place that drew them here. You could say Marks and Mathelena were smitten.

The Binkleys had money and means, so they had choices. They had friends who were travelling on to Waterloo County, and they could have stuck with their original plan and gone along with them, could have afforded to buy land there. But this place, this actual ground – its drama and distinction – spoke to them, touched their hearts. They didn't want to see what was over the next hill. What they saw here was more than enough.

DESPITE THIS WINSOME STORY of the Binkleys' arrival, Carol and Mary's binders confirm that Marks and Mathelena were not the original owners of this exact piece of land. In fact, the names of the first people to actually own this land are not commemorated in this neighbourhood. There are no street signs, schools or churches around here bearing the names of Jemima, Sarah or Mary Johnson, who owned the original deed to the series of lots purchased by the Binkleys.

There are many reasons for this absence. For one thing, Jemima, Sarah and Mary were part Hodinöhsö:ni' – part Indian, in the language of the times. Their father was Lieutenant Brant

Johnson, the half-Mohawk, half-Anglo-Irish son of the renowned and influential Sir William Johnson, British Superintendent of Indian Affairs for the Northern District, who had reigned over an extensive estate north of the Hudson River, in upstate New York. Lieutenant Johnson's daughters, therefore, were not from this region, nor did they ever live here on the edge of the Ancaster Creek valley, so there was no time when neighbours referred to this piece of land as the "Johnsons' place."

Known as Kaghneghtago and sometimes as William, their father, Brant Johnson, was born in 1742 to Elizabeth Brant, one of several Mohawk women with whom Sir William Johnson had children before establishing a long-term relationship and family with Mary (Molly) Brant, the famous and politically influential sister of Thaientané:ken, or Joseph Brant. Jemima, Sarah and Mary's mother is believed to have been the daughter of a white Virginian, captured by Western Natives and eventually returned to Sir William. She and Brant Johnson were married in the same British-style ceremony at which Joseph Brant married Margaret (better known as Peggy) Neggen Aoghyatonghsera.

Brant Johnson had inherited considerable property from his father's estate when Sir William died suddenly of a stroke in 1774, but he was forced to abandon it when he and his family, including Sir William's widow, Molly, fled the region at the outbreak of the Revolutionary War. During the war, he re-entered upstate New York as a scout with Butler's Rangers, and rose to the rank of lieutenant in what became known as the Indian Department of the British Army, fighting alongside relatives and friends such as Joseph Brant and Daniel Claus. To escape the warfare in their

Mohawk Valley home, his fair-haired daughters had accompanied Molly Brant's children to Montréal, where they received
their education.

Searching online databases for Upper Canadian land petitions
after the war, I learned how long it took for the British colonial government to compensate those who had lost properties
in America. Lieutenant Brant Johnson, for example, submitted
a first claim for losses to the British colonial commissioners in
August 1787, and his case was not resolved until 1796. His first
submission noted that he had lost one thousand acres he had
inherited from his father's estate, and an additional two thousand acres of his own, plus a house and barn where he had kept
livestock. He estimated the value of these properties at £1369.12.
The Treaty of Paris, which brought the war to a close, had been
signed in 1783, but it took until 1792 for John Graves Simcoe,
the first civilian Lieutenant Governor of the newly designated
province of Upper Canada, to formalize the system whereby
petitioners could submit requests for compensation in land to
the Executive Council.

Accordingly, the records of the Upper Canada Land Petitions
Orders in Council show that in November of that year, Lieutenant Brant Johnson submitted a petition for land to the Executive
Council in Newark (today Niagara-on-the-Lake). By this time,
Brant Johnson had a terminal illness. We know this because a
second petition a year later, this time from his daughters Jemima,
Sarah and Mary, indicates he was suffering from a "violent Rheu-
matic Complaint owing to which he has been confined to his
bed for three years last and is not likely ever to leave his Room
again." Jemima, Sarah and Mary Johnson's petition, received at

the Executive Council Office on June 8, 1793, records that their father Brant Johnson, "Lieutt of the late Six Nations Indn Dept located 800 acres land in the 8th Township near to the head of now Burlington Bay 4th & 5th Concession in the year 1785 being what was at that time allowed by Government" and that "in the year 1788, their Father again located (in consequence of an additional quantity allowed) one thousand & Fifty acres in the 9th & 10th Concessions of said Township No 8." The daughters complained that a man named Moses Morden had taken advantage of their not having a certificate for this land and had begun "an improvement although he well knew the land has ever been located upon as their property . . . having been assigned them by their Father for their further support." The Council ruled against Morden, confirming the daughters' entitlement in June that year, but apparently the exact number of acres they were to receive required further clarification, because the board received a final petition from the three women in July 1796 indicating that their father had applied for and received nineteen hundred acres and were praying "that one hundred Acres more be allowed him, being the usual allowance to officers of similar rank," and requesting an additional twelve hundred acres for each of them as his surviving dependants. The Orders in Council approved the addition of one hundred acres to the father's grant and reduced the daughter's requested twelve hundred to eight hundred acres, to "be granted individually to each of the petitioners in consideration of their personal merits." Much of what is now West Hamilton, then, was originally part of these meritorious women's land.

The popular shorthand of the settlement of Canada has settlers, with their land surveys and concepts of private property, pushing Indigenous people – who did not operate by these concepts – off their lands, and never the twain shall meet. This shorthand oversimplifies the multicultural mixing that took place between Indigenous and colonial people in early contact societies such as Upper Canada at the turn of the nineteenth century. Many whites such as Sir William Johnson and his family were deeply immersed in Iroquoian ways, and a good number of Indigenous people had integrated Western education and Christianity into their own lives. The story of the Binkleys purchasing this land from the Johnsons demonstrates how mixed the relationships in this region could be. Emerging colonial law had tried to draw strict lines between settlers and First People. So, for example, British law did not allow settlers to buy land directly from Indigenous people.

The Royal Proclamation of 1763 recognized that "great Frauds and Abuses have been committed in the purchasing Lands of the Indians, to the great Prejudice of our Interest, and to the great Dissatisfaction of the said Indians," and thenceforth insisted that the Crown broker all land negotiations with First People. It also drew what became known as the Proclamation Line along the Appalachian Mountains and St. Lawrence watershed, forbidding colonial settlement west and north of this line and preserving those territories for their Indigenous inhabitants. The British needed to make diplomatic moves like this, especially with Indigenous allies such as the Hodinöhsö:ni', in order to maintain their precarious hold on the trading regions they had recently wrested from the French, whose Native allies threatened to reverse their recent gains. You could say that Sir William Johnson's intermarriages and mixed-race family was a literal living out of this international diplomacy.

But this diplomatic necessity put British law at odds with the expansionist ambitions of American settlers, which fuelled the rebellion rising in the thirteen colonies. In a sense, we live today in the after-effects of the diplomatic doublespeak derived from the Royal Proclamation that broadcasts protection for Indigenous peoples even as it reduces them from allies upon whom the state depends to childlike wards who are not allowed to decide what to do with their own lands.

It's not possible to say conclusively how Lieutenant Brant Johnson and his children would have been categorized under British colonial law. As an officer in the Indian Department, would the lieutenant have been considered an "Indian" or a regular member of the British Army, like any other Scot, Irishman or Englishman? Would his daughters Jemima, Sarah and Mary have been considered Mohawk or British? As the children of a prominent officer who fought with the British army, they received an officer's land grant, apparently in fee simple – meaning they could sell or keep the land as they saw fit. I've seen no sign that their eventual sale to the Binkleys was ever questioned, so apparently the Royal Proclamation didn't apply to them.

Their story, therefore, inhabits the undefined, liminal zone that existed at the time. The question of whether or not grants of land to Indigenous military allies were subject to the Royal Proclamation was precisely the cause of Joseph Brant's increasing exasperation with the British colonial government. The Six Nations refugees for whom he was negotiating were trying to raise money to build homes, schools and roads by selling or leasing portions of the Haldimand Tract, the grant of land along the Grand River with which they had been compensated for their services to the British during the war. Indeed, it was for one of these portions, Block Two in Waterloo County, that Marks and Mathelena had been headed with their Lancaster County friends when they were waylaid by the escarpment vista. But the government delayed Six Nations' land sales, scratching its powdered wig as it tried to decide how and whether the Royal Proclamation applied to their displaced longhouse allies, leaving Brant and the other Hodinöhsö:ni' leaders unable to address the Grand River refugees' desperate needs. Perhaps the Johnson sisters were able to sell their land because they were not considered "Indian" on the basis that Iroquoian ancestry is traced through the mother's line rather than the father's, so their white Virginian mother would have excluded them from clan and nation membership. Perhaps, too, they followed the precedent of other Mohawk-British army officers who had served in the Indian Department – such as Joseph Brant himself, on his own private land grant in Burlington – and treated their land grants as fee-simple, private property.

Carol Binkley's page protectors include another story that shows how blurred cultural boundaries were at the Head-of-the-Lake, while Upper Canada was being formed. When the original Binkley homestead was razed, writes Miss G.L. Buttrum in a 1973 article on "The Binkley Farms" in *Ancaster's Heritage*, "an old Bible was found. Printed in 1787, it was a Mohawk translation of parts of Genesis, the Psalms, the New Testament, and the Anglican Prayerbook, translated by Captain Joseph Brant." This Bible is a telling artifact, documenting as it does the printed story of Adam and Eve that Joseph Brant had translated from English into Mohawk, and not the oral one about Atsi'tsiaká:ion on the back of the turtle, which he would have grown up with. This work, found here in the Ancaster Creek valley, reminds me of another artifact of Brant's that also lived right here. In 1856, a man named Benjamin Drew published a book called *The Refugee: Narratives of Fugitive Slaves in Canada*, which drew upon interviews he had collected from former black slaves in what is today Ontario. One of the stories he recorded was given to him by the ninety-some-year-old Sophia Pooley, who had been captured into slavery as a child in New York State and sold to none other than Captain Joseph Brant. She moved to the Head-of-the-Lake with Brant's household when he came here to take up his grant of land in Burlington. She was later sold to Samuel Hatt of Ancaster before receiving her freedom in her later years and moving to Waterloo. She could remember hearing the Battle of Stoney Creek during the War of 1812, and recalled hunting for deer with Joseph Brant's children, Peggy, Mary, Katy, Joseph and Jacob, right where Spencer Creek runs into Cootes Paradise.

This ground contains more complexity than our abbreviated histories tend to admit. The story of the transfer of this land, from Indigenous territory to settlers' farms, is not a simple story of white settlers directly appropriating Indigenous land. The overall result is the same, but the actual process by which this Dish With One Spoon was pieced and parcelled into private property passes through a blurry period of cultural mixing, interracial marriage, political alliance-building and military allyship. And all of it characterized by syncretism and acculturation. As a result, the first people to assert possession of this land as their own private property were fair-haired British-Mohawk Anglicans, whose father had fought with the British Army and whose grandfather

had been a baronet in the colonial aristocracy. Sir William Johnson had been the largest slaveholder in Britain's northern district
in America with ninety African slaves, and both Brant Johnson
and Joseph Brant had grown up in his household seeing slaves
as natural parts of daily life. It's hard to draw clear lines in
circumstances like these: Hodinöhsö:ni' people had the ancient
practice of adopting those they had conquered into their own
families, and all family members were assigned responsibilities
to carry out the necessary labour that kept the family going. So
when Sophia Pooley says she was adopted into Brant's family, but
was later sold to Samuel Hatt for one hundred dollars, was she
treated as an adopted daughter, some kind of servant, or a slave?

The presence of Sophia Pooley and of Joseph Brant's Mohawk
Bible on this land flies in the face of the myth of Canada being
established by white settlers, and the presence of the Binkleys chal-
lenges the myth of it being settled by Loyalist Britons. Instead,
members of a Mohawk-Anglican slave-owning family sold this
land to German-speaking Pennsylvanians, not United Empire
Loyalists, whose father had served as an officer in the American
army. That's who "settled" this west end of the City of Hamilton.

I WONDER IF THE Binkleys had the same battles I do with troubling goings-on in the ground? It's becoming a regular occurrence.
I'll come out the back door on a fine spring morning, stretch and
yawn in the warm sunlight bouncing off the pines and maples,
and just as I'm getting into one of those blisses that made Mathelena ask Marks to stop here, I'll see that those critters have been

rolling up my Kentucky blue like it's old carpet headed for the dump.

Some people hate raccoons. Not me. I like their Lone Ranger masks, their alert and perky ears. But when they roll up my grass, I curse their little opposable thumbs. They're handier than we are, with their four hands compared to our two. A couple of those bandits working overnight can roll up and mound your entire backyard. Did they dig up Marks's new spring wheat, too? Did they unearth Mathelena's carrot seedlings or potatoes?

Wendy and I reduced the size of the lawn in our backyard significantly when we built the addition on the back of the house. Then we expanded the perimeter flower gardens, the flagstone patios and the walkways, all of which took out more lawn. All that remains now, within view of the Binkley family cemetery, is a small strip of grass ten feet wide by twenty-five feet long. It's what we were aiming for: a tiny patch of lawn just big enough for a game of bocce ball, or for little kids to run off steam. It makes the toes happy, but it's still small enough that we don't need to water or use fertilizer. I can mow it in five minutes. This remainder of a lawn may be miniscule, but that just makes it feel all the more precious to me.

So my blood's been brought to a boil many mornings these past few years, when I step out the back door and see they've been at it again. Great rolls of sod lie in clumps and hillocks around the lawn, steam rising from the black undersoil in the morning sun, green blades underneath already starting to wilt.

Why are these night raiders tearing up our lawn? What are they digging for? I pull up the internet and learn that they are looking for white grubs, which emerge just after the larval stage of European chafers, June beetles and Japanese beetles, and their favourite food is the roots of lawn grass. I've seen them before, when I cut sod to dig out the shape of the patios, but back then I didn't know what I was looking at. The grubs look a bit like bloated caterpillars about three-quarters of an inch long – that is, if you stretch them out. Any I've seen are always curled in a horse-shoe – they make me think of a cross between a termite and a shrimp. They have the beginnings of an insect's six legs at the front of their body, and there's a bit of orange colouring in their heads, while the rest of their body is a sickly white. These fat, greasy-looking worms must be about as tasty as prawns on the tongues of raccoons, skunks and northern flickers. They're so delicious that these hunters will go to any length to collect them. During the cold weather, the grubs dig down below the frost line to stay warm, but once the spring thaw arrives, they climb back near the surface where the grass roots are. Again, when summer's heat dries out the soil, they descend to lower, damp earth, and they don't resurface again until the fall, when mild temperatures and rain return.

The result is that my lawn is under attack from both above and below, every spring and every fall. The mandibles below attract the mandibles above. Last year, this in-ground contest destroyed my darling patch of grass. Although the grubs come close to the surface only in mild weather, the damage didn't show as much in the spring, when there was plenty of rain to green the rootless grass. But when it got hot in July, big patches of dead lawn spread like mange across the yard.

I hate watering the lawn. I think grass should be grass: green when it's wet and brown when it's not. And so long as we've lived

here we haven't used chemicals on it. We don't want to put unknown residue into the ecosystem. If Marks and Mathelena and
all those Binkleys could raise farm produce here without artificial supports, surely I can raise a bit of grass. But the mange
continued to spread. The situation called for desperate measures,
so I put on the sprinkler morning and evening, well into August.
I spread blizzards of non-chemical eco-fertilizer, trying to keep
the grass from dying. I was fighting a losing battle. Every day,
more yellow patches. Every morning, new chunks of lawn, uprooted and dying. I was at my wit's end. The grubs were supposed
to have gone away by now, dug down deep in the hot, dry summer. But maybe the raccoons and skunks had got into a digging
habit, and even in July they couldn't stop, curious to see, once
again, if there were grubs to eat. The situation made me want to
buy a shotgun.

One website said that you can scare off lawn-rolling animals
with a water sprinkler activated by a motion detector, so I ran out
and got one. Every evening, I'd step outside, screw this contraption onto the end of our garden hose, stomp it into the ground
and turn on the tap. The sprinkler would sit, spiked into the
ground, potent as a loaded gun. Wendy loved this part, because
the minute I turned on the water, my movements would trigger
the sprinkler. I'd be doing a Charlie Chaplin, capering across the
yard, jerking to a halt when the water swept by me, then sprinting to the safety of the back door.

It sort of worked. One evening, I watched a big raccoon star-
tle when he lumbered into the yard and the sprinkler fired up. I
don't think he was too worried about getting wet. It was just that
the thing kept startling him. He'd be jetted for five seconds, and

then it would stop. He'd move a muscle and the water cannon would hit him again. After two or three blasts of water, I think he just gave up, deciding to try someone else's lawn, where he didn't get a water shot every time he flexed a limb.

Thereafter, the only parts of the lawn that continued to get dug up were out of reach of the sprinkler. I could never attach the mechanism to the hose tightly enough, and I felt guilty about the water that dripped from the connection through the night. The disappointing thing is that, despite the way the sprinkler scared off skunks and raccoons, the yellow patches of dying grass continued to spread. I may have found a solution to the problem above ground, but the underground foragers still eluded me.

I returned to the internet. The solution proposed for taking care of the root-eaters under the surface felt to me both scientific and mystical. If I didn't want to pour chemicals onto my yard to kill the grubs underneath – which I didn't and don't – I needed nematodes. According to the website and the fellow I talked to at the garden centre, these microscopic beings eat grubs. They are tiny as bacteria, and they burrow into the soft membranes of the grubs down in the dark earth, eating them from the inside like parasites in tree rot or warbles on the soft back of a deer or cow.

Like a lot of science, laypeople like me have to take it on faith, as it's invisible to the naked eye.

The nematodes I bought came in a plastic egg the size of a tennis ball that had to be kept in the fridge until I was ready to spray them onto the ground. When I unscrewed the two hemispheres of the egg, I found inside a three-inch square bag filled with what looked and felt like damp, fine clay – or like cumin or ginger powder. The instructions said to put the clay in a hose-end sprayer and mix it with a couple of cups of lukewarm water. I opened the bag and could see no signs of life. The nematodes smelled earthy – more like clay than cumin.

The instructions also said that the ground has to be moist and warm for the nematodes to do their parasitic work. If the ground is dry or hard, or if it's too cold, they just die on the surface and don't sink in and reach their targets. So I waited for an out-of-character rainy day late in August and, with the ground squelching under my heels, unrolled the garden hose. I poured the cumin powder from the egg into the canister of my sprayer and whipped it into a beige soup. Next, I walked around the yard for a good half hour, spraying back and forth and up and down, watching the beige line sink in the see-through canister. Finally, the canister was empty, and I had to commit to keeping the lawn damp for two weeks. The idea was to soak the nematodes down into the grass roots. Trying not to think about water bills, I kept the sprinkler going for a half hour morning and evening for the next fortnight.

No sign of change.

The motion-detector sprayer was keeping the skunks and raccoons away, but the dead yellow patches continued to grow. The unseen grubs must still have been eating the roots. Maybe the nematodes had died. Maybe nematodes were a scam and someone down in Florida was laughing their way to the bank. Maybe the ground hadn't been wet enough. Maybe watering morning and evening wasn't enough. How would I know? What was happening in the pillow of the ground was beyond me. The whole process was a mystery that took place under ground, exactly where I couldn't investigate, unless I wanted to start digging up the turf I myself was trying to save. It's hard to build a relationship with reality when the realities you're trying to relate to are out of sight.

To tell the truth, I just gave up. I'd done everything I could think of, except use insecticides, and I'd be damned if I was going to resort to chemicals whose after-effects might remain in the ground for who knows how long. The truth is, I had started to worry about the nematodes. They were supposed to kill off the white grubs, but what would they do to helpful underground creatures, such as earthworms? Do nematodes know the difference between a grub and an earthworm? Or do they eat one and all? My neighbour's a scientist, and he assured me these nematodes are victim specific. They dig into just one kind of creature, not all kinds. They're not omnivores. But I still wasn't sure. How do the makers of bags of nematodes know this, I wonder? Might a nematode get tired of a single, eternal diet and dive into a juicy earthworm or a springtail instead?

That's the trouble with trying to understand the land we humans live upon. We can only imagine what happens underneath: whether it's what nematodes eat, or what happens to ground water, or how decay is part of all life, human and non-human, it all happens in the dark and out of sight. The ferment underground is a dense interaction of all the elements that make up the entire biography of this place, and that ferment creates the life that's happening here every day. It's all a mystery, so most of the time, we go on faith, or depend on what others have told us. Sometimes momentary signs poke up from underground, get posted on gravestones, street signs and schools in neighbourhoods, but what's under there gets turned only briefly to the light before being buried once again.

DID THE WHITE GRUBS chew the roots of the wheat or barley or cabbages that Marks and Mathelena Binkley planted here after they bought lots fifty-three to fifty-seven of the Johnson sisters' lands in 1800? Maybe not. These are the larvae of *European* chafers and *Japanese* beetles, after all, and perhaps those insect stowaways had not yet arrived on this continent. We do know that the Binkleys began to clear the maple, hickory, pine and oak woods along the Ancaster Creek ravine, and that they erected the log house where Brant's Mohawk Bible was later found. On the southern slope of the ravine, they built the first tannery at the Head-of-the-Lake in 1801, and in 1802 they moved out of the log house into a newly constructed frame house. Starting from scratch like that must have been demanding, often frustrating work. I'm sure that skunks and racoons were the least of their worries.

Marks lived only long enough at what became known as Binkley's Hollow to see his family establish their shelter and launch their farm and leather businesses. He died in 1805, one of the first to be lowered into the ground below the white pines in the cemetery back of our yard. None other than the rebel journalist William Lyon Mackenzie admired the enterprise and high-mindedness of the Binkleys, who spoke German at home and English with others. Mackenzie wrote in *Sketches of Canada and the United States* that Marks died without leaving an official will, which meant that his property fell automatically to his eldest son, John. But the dying father had spoken with John about dividing the land equally between himself and his two brothers, George and William. MacKenzie prized John's integrity in carrying out his father's wishes to the letter, John staying on at the original homestead and the tannery, while William took the

section on the western side of the Hollow and George the eastern side. Because land titles passed down to men, it's less clear
what happened to their sisters, but it's believed they married local
men: Catherine to a Mr. Hughson of Hamilton, and Elizabeth to
a Mr. van Duzer of Stoney Creek. Sarah, meanwhile, married a
Mr. Rees Tunis of West Flamborough.

In 1898, at age seventy-three, Henry Binkley, Marks and
Mathelena's grandson, retold family stories of those early days.
He recalled the gooseflesh he felt under his blankets as a boy,
listening to the night sounds of wolves, bears and wildcats in the
ravine. When he grew up to inherit William's farm, he built a large
brick home atop the northern slope of the Hollow overlooking a
water trough on the road below. Predators must have declined as
a threat, as that trough quenched the thirst of untroubled horses
for over a hundred years, until car traffic straightened and wid-
ened the road in 1965. In 1847, on the east side of the valley,
George's son Jacob (1809–1867) built the handsome stone house
that still stands at the north end of Binkley Road, just around
the corner from here. Even in his time, however, horses were not
safe, and Jacob assembled an Association for the Detecting of
Horse Thieves, which recovered three to ten horses a year. Jacob's
stately home was called Lakelet Vale after the spring-fed pond
one level down in the ravine behind it. Bink's Pond, as it was
dubbed, filled the imaginations, and the hours, of generations
of children who grew up on this end of Hamilton with fishing,
swimming and skating. I've seen pictures of people skating there
in 1917. There was even a hockey team. The pond was bulldozed
in the late 1960s, however, when McMaster University paved
most of Binkley's Hollow for parking lots. While the pond no

longer exists, the springs do, and they feed the deer who forage in what I call the deer yard down below our neighbourhood.

In 1860, Jacob's son Jacob George built a stone Drive House on the lip of the ravine beside his father's grand stone house. Its upper storey housed carriages and implements, as well as a carpenter and blacksmith shop. The lower part consisted of a wine cellar with an arched brick ceiling. A *Globe and Mail* report on the Agricultural Exhibition in Hamilton on September 21, 1860, praises Mr. Binkley's fine fruit and grape wine in addition to the sherry he made from local currants. From his nursery of fruit trees and vineyards, Jacob George made what the newspaper called "invalid wine" that he sold as far east as Halifax. I've never been able to find out what would make a wine invalid. Perhaps it has something to do with not having a license to produce or sell it? Or, was it good medicine for invalids?

So the Binkleys settled and thrived on the Johnson lands. Carol Binkley's carefully sorted family trees record thirteen children for John and his wife, Nancy Gingrich; six for his younger brother George and wife, Magdalene Bechtel; and nine for the youngest brother, William, and his wife, Barbara Baringer. It wasn't long before Marks and Mathelena had over one hundred great-grandchildren. Their children's children's children spread across a series of districts in what's now the Hamilton-Wentworth region. The Binkleys intermarried with other families in the area whose names are listed on the street signs on this end of town – Bowman, Horning, Smith and Cottrill. Each of these names appears in the Marks Binkley Cemetery on Lakelet Drive as well as in the Henry Binkley Family Cemetery on the west side of Binkley's Hollow at the end of Desjardins Avenue.

Daniel Coleman

One spring day, I hiked across the valley and stood in the scent of new-mown grass on the upland of the Henry Binkley Family Cemetery. No sign of underground root-eaters here. The grounds crew must know more than I do about nematodes – or they use insecticides. Ancaster Creek muttered along its course sixty feet down at the bottom of the treed slope. I felt a shiver as I leaned toward the headstones of Henry (1825–1907) and Marilla (nee Smith, 1829–1919) Binkley and read the names of seven of their children who are buried there. Hiram (1855–1930) lived a full life, but the other six didn't make it out of their teens. They must have had sickness run through the family, because three children died in 1865: Barbara at thirteen years old, Mary at eleven and William at five. Can you imagine? I paced slowly along the front of the thirty markers surrounded by the low stone cemetery walls and learned that Mary Jane, wife of Elijah Binkley, also lost three of her four children in one year: William Henry at eleven, Eliza Jane at nine and David Marshall at two – all in 1860. Carol and Mary's binders explain that the children died of scarlet fever. Two years later, Mary herself died giving birth to George Macklem, who also did not survive.

All that grief, right here in this ground. Rather than a pillow of peace, this ground turns and turns in a ferment of tears and sorrow.

Despite these devastating losses, the Binkleys thrived. By 1815, there were enough children to build a stone schoolhouse on a piece of their farm that fronted the Dundas Road, now Main Street, between the intersections with Westbourne and West Park streets. It was replaced by a brick schoolhouse in 1880. I've seen a photo of the brick one, with its belfry and separate entrances for boys and girls. It looks a lot like a church, which is exactly what it functioned as part-time. They even called it Binkley Church, as Sunday school and worship services were led by Methodist or Presbyterian ministers there, depending on who was available.

By the early twentieth century, J. Allen Binkley owned Jacob's farm. He and his sister, Mrs. M. E. Rasberry – spelled without the *p* – offered some land on the Dundas Road one hundred metres east of the school, where a separate church could be built. They asked that it be named Binkley Union Church. When it opened in 1912, seven Binkleys were listed among the sixty-three founding members. Six years later, the church members signed the Basis of Union that amalgamated the Presbyterian, Methodist and Congregational churches into the United Church of Canada. It took a hundred years for the Binggelis or Pinckleys to become Binckleys in Pennsylvania, and another hundred in Canada for them to become Binkleys, whose German-speaking Reform heritage had amalgamated so successfully into Canada's mainstream that they were pretty much British-Canadians in their neighbours' minds.

It's easy to look around today at this neighbourhood, with its red brick houses, lawns and gardens, and forget this was once the farm of Pennsylvania Dutch. There are a few reminders of their old grounds, such as the huge and scarred weeping willow that still stands across the street from our house – the last of seven that once lined a drive on Jacob Binkley's farm. Dr. Mark F. Binkley was the last Binkley to own property on the old Hollow, and when he died in 1958 at age ninety-one, his land was purchased by Loblaw Groceterias and turned into the commercial zone where a strip mall now occupies the southeast corner of the junction at Main, Wilson and Osler Streets. The signs on streets, the church and the now-converted school are the remaining reminders of the family's presence here. Those, and the cemetery stones tipped up from the earth, marking the many Binkleys whose love for this place, whose accumulation of grief and tragedy, and whose energy and toil, shaped and sculpted the contours of the ground we live upon.

THERE'S SOMETHING CALM AND deep about learning what I can about the changing ground on which I live. This, despite the fact that the earth and its workings remain, ultimately, beyond the reach of my inquiries. I still don't know who or what made the six-inch tunnel under our patio, though it had to be some kind of living being. I don't know if the Johnson sisters ever saw or cared to see this land that had so captured Mrs. Binkley's heart. I don't know why the nematodes didn't stop the grubs from eating the roots of my lawn. So this feeling of depth and calm doesn't come from certitude. It has more to do with opening to the life – the many lives – turning and turning in the earth. We humans know there's a lot going on beneath our feet. The basic ground keeps us upright every day – and, according to our stories of origin, its dirt is what we ourselves are made of. It's our fundament. Ultimately, it demands our reverence, but it does so quietly, since its contents and workings are always out of sight and remote from what we confidently know. Maybe that's *why* it demands veneration. I've heard Hodinöhsö:ni' elders say that the land we walk upon is made up of the faces not only of those who preceded us but of those who are yet to come. We should therefore place our feet reverently on such a peopling earth.

So should we spray the nematodes onto the ground or not? What impact do they have on the complex of living and dying, degeneration and regeneration, that's happening under our feet?

If our stories of beginnings become built up where we can see them, like the cliffs of the escarpment, so too must the stories we can't see down in the ground. The forces in the earth compete, from underneath and from above. They eat each other, become absorbed in each other, form a compost tea. In one story, this dirt was brought up from the dark sea by the humble muskrat. Later, it was laid down smooth in lakebeds before being cut up and scraped by huge sheets of ice. It retains memories of peace and violence. Yet again, this ground was a Dish With One Spoon, where game, water and rich soil fed warring and peaceful neighbours alike. It got plotted and parcelled by immigrants, soldiers and speculators – both Indigenous and European. It's been a farm, a family of farms, a tannery and a winery, a place to stop and rest after many months, even years, of wandering. It's become a neighbourhood, a suburb, a piece of city. The layers are darker and denser at the top where the decay of those who died most recently wriggles with emerging life.

I'm learning it takes years just to scratch the surface. It's not just a matter of finding out the names for European chafers or whoever dug the mystery tunnel. And it's not just knowing the stories of the people who lived here before me, from Mrs. Forbes and her family to the British Mohawks or the Pennsylvania Dutch, to the Attawandaron who knew this valley and the marsh we call Cootes Paradise. If becoming grounded means relating to the realities of this place, then it's going to involve figuring out *how* to learn, how to notice things we've been taught to ignore, to rename and forget. How will we actually make some sense out of what's right here in – and out – of plain sight?

Watershed

Only low in the land does
the water flow. It goes
to seek the level that is lowest.
– Wendell Berry, "The Book of Camp Branch"

I HAVE BEEN TRACKING water. Or, maybe I should say *trying* to track water. It's not easy to do, because water is shy. Given its own way, it shrinks from attention, sinks out of sight. Yes, there are exceptions when it's forced into dramatic displays, when underground pressure shoots it into the air in Yellowstone Park, when wind whips it into a hurricane or when the escarpment running through this city causes it to leap out at Niagara Falls. These moments of drama emphasize the retiring ways of water, which flees before the force of others.

I had never thought of trying to track water until I was confounded by that perfectly round hole running out from under our patio and beneath our lawn. I still don't know whether it was dug by animal, runoff rain or something else. That mystery hole put the question in my mind: *Where does the water go?* Without a place to begin or end – and with so many places to look – it's hard to know where to start. So never mind the Great Lakes. Never mind Lake Ontario and the rain that falls across our city. Let me start with what I can see in this yard: *What happens to the rain that falls right here?*

It's no surprise that it seeps into the soil. It rinses the air of dust and pollen and whatever else is airborne. It washes onto grass blades and tree leaves before threading its way into the earth. Where there isn't leaves and soil, it batters hard surfaces such as patio stones or the asphalt shingle roof, raising bouncing crowns of wet with each drop. Then it feels around hard objects, looking for a way down – always down. Washing pine needles and maple keys from the roof, it rushes into eavestroughs, rolls down rain gutters and gushes into our two water barrels, where it is captured – briefly. A few days later, I bucket it off to flowerpots and gardens, this rain getting rerouted from its course. You could say it gets managed.

Interesting word, "managed." It comes from the Latin word "manus," or hand. This portion of our roof rain gets handled, literally. The handle on the bucket indents my palm as I lug rainwater from the barrels to the pots of impatiens and begonias, or the concrete planter of herbs that runs along our front porch. It also gets pailed around to plants we've newly transplanted, while they're still groping their infant roots into the soil. But once those roots have sunk deep enough, they don't need this manhandled water. They can find it on their own.

The rain that spatters on the patio stones, however, does not get handled. Instead, it feels around each stone, through the screenings and gravel substrate, and into the soil below. Some of it, I surmise from the stones that collapsed by the addition, searches its way into subterranean cavities, carrying away my hard-packed, hard-won gravel. It undoes what I had done.

Some of the water that lands on the soft surfaces of my yard creeps, at varying rates, into the soil, and there it encounters millions and billions of root fibres. I've been turning over black earth, digging up overgrown and invasive plants in the garden – white goose-necked loosestrife, for example, and creeping charlie – and I can never get over the wriggling universe of roots that crowd under the surface, galaxies of tiny hairs, each seeking moisture. I look around at this single yard, with its white pines, softwood maples and red oak towering overhead. There's the grass of the lawn, the cedar and euonymus hedges, the boxwoods, Japanese maples, ferns, phlox, peonies, hostas, spiderwort, clematis, climbing roses, hydrangeas, coralbells, shasta daisies and echinacea. Each one of these plants depends upon a Milky Way of underground roots that draws secret water from the ground before passing it up, transformed into air.

What's happening is sixth-grade science, but to me it is still completely absorbing. I remember being enthralled by the illustration in my science textbook of how water's surface tension forms an elasticity so strong that it creeps, like an inchworm, up the capillaries of plants in stubborn contradiction to Newton's law of universal gravitation. The science book explained that water has strong attractions: it has cohesion, meaning that its molecules are attracted to each other; and it has adhesion, which means they are attracted to other materials, too, including not just plant fibre, but also wood, paper, soil and even glass. If the adhesion is stronger than the cohesion, then the water molecules will be attracted to the sides of the container they are in (in our present case, the capillaries in plants), which causes the water's edges to climb a bit higher than its surface in the middle of the tube. This movement forms what the textbook illustration labelled a "concave meniscus" – a sag that the water's cohesion wants to correct. The resulting relaxation of the meniscus allows adhesion to climb the capillary sides once again, just a tiny bit, which creates a new concave, and so the process repeats itself as the water inches up the tiny tube. By this means, water in the soil climbs all one hundred and fifty feet to the top of the oak growing at the back of our yard, with no pump at the bottom, just by means of adhesion and cohesion, driven by the principle that no molecule be left alone or behind. Water's fierce solidarity, according to the United States Geological Survey, provides enough oomph to not only climb the trunk of a large oak tree, like this one, but to also sweat as many as one hundred fifty thousand litres of groundwater from the undersides of its millions of leaves back into the air over the course of a year.

Water gets up into the sky, therefore, because it bonds. Because it bonds, it moves. It picks up nutrients along the way and feeds them to plants, to the air. Water is paradoxical this way, because it's both bound and free. It sticks together, but because it does so, it eludes confinement. It takes the shapes of its containers, but is not defined by them. It may be channelled for a bit, delayed in my rain barrels, but it will always seek a way out – an escape. It sticks to itself, then it dissipates. Vanishes into vapour, into thin air, a holy ghost.

IF YOU WANT TO trace the comings and goings of raccoons or coyotes, you poke at their scat to see what they're eating. Or you put a radio collar on them and watch their movements on your computer screen. If you want to track the migration of ducks or hawks, you loop a metal band around one of their legs and count them when they return. But how does a person track water? Have you ever done that schoolroom science experiment on how capillaries work? You put red food colouring in some water and place the stem of a white carnation in the mix. Soon, you see tinges of red following the veins up the stem and fanning out in the white petals, like bloodshot eyes. But colouring or tagging the water that sinks into my yard would not help track it. Slow seepage through soil cleans the water, so the colour would be sieved out somewhere in the ground.

It's not just amateurs like me who find the path of water mysterious. Even professionals like Mark Sproule-Jones from McMaster University, who has studied water in this region his whole career, finds it a tricky business. He admits that experts like himself generally approach water "in the light of scientific and engineering uncertainties." Uncertainties are especially true of groundwater, unlike the damp you see on the surface. Another professional water researcher, Linda Nolan, says that it's hard to tell what happens to groundwater, that scientists don't have a ready grasp on what it's doing and where it's going.

When water vanishes into the ground, it runs into the aquifer, made up of the geological layers beneath us that contain both solid and spongy parts. The impermeable sections consist of rock such as granite or quartzite that water can't pass through, while the porous areas are sand or gravel – or rock such as limestone, with its cracks and fissures. Surface water sinks into the soil at various rates depending on how porous the aquifer: water seeps quickly through sand or gravel, more slowly through clay. Where it cannot find a path, water collects in the spaces between particles and fissures.

In some places in the world, the aquifer is so porous that whole underground rivers never appear on the surface. The unseen conditions in any aquifer determine the water table. It depends on how far the solid rock lets the water sink, how deep or shallow the permeable sections are, how much water is soaking down from the surface and at what rate. No wonder groundwater is hard to predict: its presence depends not only on how solid or leaky the underground layers are, but also on how they settle and shift. If a crack opens in a rock somewhere down below, then everything could change. If frost or digging a basement or geothermal heat causes a new fissure, what had been an underground trickle or even a lake might emerge elsewhere as a spring, a geyser, a hot spring.

These dynamics happen – all of them – when we're not looking. I try to predict my backyard water's likely journey through the ground by trying to read the topography of slopes, depressions and crevices on and below our little plot of land on the lip of the Ancaster Creek valley, once known as Binkley's Hollow.

The flat square of the top part of our yard is not natural, but the result of the construction of our house back in the 1940s. Once the basement was dug and the foundation built, this yard would have been levelled off, sloping gradually away from the house toward the two-foot-high retaining wall sixty feet from our back door. This levelling was adjusted and repeated six years ago, after we dug the new basement for the addition we built on the back of our house. Our new back door is now fifteen feet closer to the retaining wall. Once the construction crew left, I took a two-by-four and used it as a long blade to level off the soil, again sloping it away from the house. Then I built the stone patios, before Wendy and I replanted the gardens and lawn.

We knew that before everything else you have to think about water. Which we couldn't see but had to imagine as best we could.

So, if the rainwater follows my imagination, any runoff that doesn't soak into the garden and get sucked up by roots will drip over, or – more likely – seep under, the retaining wall, heading downhill into the part of our property that drops into Ancaster Creek valley below. The back half of our property is deeply shaded by a fringe of Carolinian forest – maples, pines and that huge northern red oak. There's also a second canopy closer to the ground, where ostrich and maidenhair ferns, solomon's seal, red and white trilliums, trout lilies, jewel weed, pachysandra and periwinkle make a dark ground cover. The result is that the soil on this slope is always cool and damp. I've lifted a pinch or two to my nose and smelled how fresh it is, even on hot summer days after weeks of no rain. Water gets here. It drips from the leaves of the upper canopy when it rains, and it slips off those of the second canopy, closer to the earth, where it joins the seepage from our yard above.

But that's about the best I could do in figuring out the ways of water. So I thought I should get help from someone who knows more about these things. I called the Hamilton Conservation Authority, and a woman with the wonderful name of Cherish, who works on their Watershed Stewardship campaign, drove over to give me a free consultation about what's happening with the water in my yard.

"I'm a complete novice," I told her over the phone. "I'd like a professional assessment."

When she got here, she surprised me by starting where I had: she took note of the hard surfaces – the roof, the water barrels, the stone patio. Then she concentrated on the ground. She got out her soil sample auger, which looks like a tiny version of a manual post-hole digger, with a round and pointed hollow blade for twisting down into the earth. The *T* at the top of its three-foot wooden handle lets you grab each end and lean on it with your bodyweight, then give it a big wide turn. We drilled down eighteen inches into the lawn at the back of the house. It was not difficult to dig down through the first eight inches of black topsoil, but it took more muscle to turn the auger once we hit the next layer of fine clay mixed with sand.

"Good drainage here," Cherish said as she laid out the vertical column of earth that had collected in the hollow tube of her auger. Examining the column on the grass, she fingered each of the sedimentary layers in order. "This dark eight inches is your topsoil. This is beautiful stuff. Rich and moist. Light, too, and a bit mealy. No wonder your gardens are booming." She gave an encouraging smile. "Now, see this next tan-coloured section? It's mostly clay. When it's moist, it holds its shape, but when you break it apart and rub it in your palm like this, it turns to powder. But see these crystal grains? Those are sand. The sand breaks up the clay and lets the water through.

"Now, the thing to do is to look for orange chunks like this," she broke open a clump of clay with her thumb and turned over some quarter-inch, carrot-coloured blobs. "Oxidation creates these. It shows water has sat here for a while. I'm guessing the clay gets denser deeper down, with less sand in it, so moisture gets blocked. Anyway, you don't have many orange clumps in this soil, and they're small, so water doesn't stay here long. Most of it either drains down through the clay and sand, or it runs off the surface."

She slipped a lock of her auburn hair behind her ear, picked up her auger and headed down the back slope into the strip of woods below our retaining wall. There, I watched as she dug a second core sample down near our property line in the dark shade. This time, the auger sank right down, almost without effort. Cherish laid out the substrate again: eight or ten inches of cool black topsoil, but this time mostly sand, and very little clay underneath.

"You can do a taste test," Cherish said. "You'll feel the grit of the sand in your teeth, compared to the powder of the clay."

I put a pinch on my tongue. She was right. The sand crunched in my molars, while the powder of the clay tasted dry and a little bitter.

At the bottom of the slope, we found no orange deposits at all, so the water must run through this soil even more quickly than it does through the lawn above. Cherish wasn't sure what would make for the difference in soil types, but she shared my guess that the yard above was made from clay infill lifted up from ten or twelve feet down, when they dug the basement for the house. At the bottom of our hill, the slope in the shade is closer to the limestone bones under the valley's lip. To get here, water sinks through topsoil, through sand, and, once it hits the porous limestone, it finds cracks and holes and runs who knows where.

GROUNDWATER PLAYS HIDE AND seek. On the footpath below the slope where Cherish took the last soil sample and above the university maintenance building down in the valley, water trickles into several little low spots. The deer paths in the valley lead from one of those spots to the next, a series of water fountains for wildlife. There's one below the northeast corner of the Marks Binkley Cemetery. There's another below my neighbour's house east of us, and a bigger branched basin that whispers along the eastern edge of the parking lot below. With all three, I can stand in the scented shade of maples and walnuts, where the water gathers, and look uphill to the trench that marks where each emerges. But if you walk along our street up top, with its sealed asphalt and concrete sidewalks flanked by flattened lawns, you won't see why or how the water finds the gullies now, let alone how it created or claimed them in the past.

These tiny downhill seeps are called non-point source water, whose origins you can't pinpoint. Does the water run off the surface above into the earth for thirty or forty metres and resurface here? Or do these moss-edged springs rise from underground cracks that bring this seepage from farther away? With the crumbling limestone of the Niagara Escarpment system all around here, the broken understructure could allow water to follow a seam a long way from its source. The concept of a point source assumes the world of plumbing, the idea that if you want to know where the water running out the end of a pipe comes from, you look for where that pipe starts.

But in nature, how do you find the beginning of the pipe? Water ripples out of the ground below our place to become these three little trickles that aren't big enough to be brooks or creeks. Perhaps I should call them rills. They have considerable flow when we've had recent rain and are reduced to damp seeps during dry spells. Although I can spot where the water shows up for each one, I don't think I can call these rills point sources. The water comes from somewhere else, but where? Uphill in our neighbours' yards? Somewhere in the aquifer underneath the city?

Non-point sources: it's a name that points to what we don't know.

People like groundwater to stay in the ground – out of sight and out of the way of the structures we build, such as parking lots, roads, sidewalks and buildings. Thus, all three rills have been drained into concrete and metal culverts that return the recently surfaced water back into the dark almost as soon as it finds daylight. These seeps get submerged under the sealed surfaces of the university's asphalt parking lots and its scattering of maintenance and other buildings.

"They should never have built those buildings down there anyway," says my neighbour Mark. "They're low in the water table, and they have constant problems with wet floors and sewer backups."

It's true. Those parking lots and buildings were constructed over the flood plain that fans out around Ancaster Creek, after it's joined by Sulphur Creek and before it merges with Spencer Creek just a few hundred metres down the valley. Some maps call the first two combined streams Coldwater Creek, because when you place a thermometer in it in summer, the water registers below twenty degrees Celsius, which allows for certain kinds of fish and other creatures to live in it. Other maps just call it Ancaster Creek all the way until it runs into Spencer Creek. With the amount of city runoff artificially warmed on streets, sidewalks and university parking lots, I wonder if the temperature is pushing this twenty-degree limit.

Much of the area must have been too marshy for the Binkleys to farm after they arrived here from Pennsylvania in 1800, as this valley appears largely untouched, even after the farm turned into city blocks. I once heard someone say they found an old apple tree down here, but you don't see clusters of orchard survivors like you do in other ravines around the city.

This flood plain became part of the land managed by the Royal Botanical Gardens, after the gardens were established in the 1930s. The RBG laid out a system of walking trails and an arboretum below the Marks Binkley Cemetery, where visitors could amble down to the creek through the reeds and willows. I've seen a map from the early 1960s that outlines what it calls the Coldspring Valley Trails. It shows that where the maintenance building is today was, back then, a pond or marsh. One of my neighbours, Glenn, grew up on this street, and he remembers tour buses parking on Lakelet Drive in front of the cemetery and flooding passengers into the trail system below.

Lakelet Drive and Lakelet Vale, the latter the name Jacob Binkley gave the grand stone house he built in 1847. This water, seeping out along this slope, defined this place for its first farming family.

But when the university took over this end of the valley from the RBG in the mid-1960s, it covered much of the valley floor in asphalt. The original creek was bulldozed and forced into a channel on the west margin of the valley. Binkley Pond, the old swimming hole farther west along the valley, was erased, and the many little non-point rills that fed the flood plain were piped and buried. After draining the place, the land was scraped flat for huge parking lots, baseball diamonds and a landing pad for the university hospital helicopter. I've walked along the channelized Ancaster Creek on the other side of the valley, where the RBG trails once were, and I've seen where the runoff pipes stick out from under the acres of asphalt, draining water from these rills and the tarmac into the creek. For much of the year, it is oily and warm. In winter, it's salty.

These drainpipes and channelized creek, then, are where the runoff from our yard goes on its way to Cootes Paradise, Hamilton Harbour, Lake Ontario, the St. Lawrence River and finally the Atlantic Ocean.

Or it was until recently.

OVER THE PAST TEN years, the City of Hamilton has been searching for better ways to manage stormwater runoff. The old part of the city below the escarpment uses what's known as a combined sewer system. The combined system chutes stormwater from street and parking lot drains into the same pipes that pump household and industrial sewage through the city's six hundred kilometres of piping to the Woodward Avenue Wastewater Treatment Plant. There it gets sieved, rested, stirred and resettled from pond to pond. City workers spend long days skimming condoms, tampons, dental floss, baby wipes and syringes floating in the water Hamiltonians flush down their drains. Gradually, through this process, the water is relieved of its burdens until it's clear again. Only then is it released into Hamilton Harbour.

The problem with this combined system is that heavy downpours can swamp the pumps and pipes, overwhelm the system and spill untreated water, inevitably, into Cootes Paradise and Hamilton Harbour. The culverts and drainpipes under the university parking lots are part of the network of drains that spill into Ancaster Creek, which of course runs into Cootes Paradise, and from there into Hamilton Harbour and eventually Lake Ontario, where our city's drinking water intakes can be found.

This is what happens when you follow water. You start with raindrops on the roof and pretty soon you're talking about condoms in your drinking water. Because it's all one water. Contaminated water is an old problem in Hamilton, one that recalls the cholera epidemics of the nineteenth century. The crowded and unsanitary conditions on immigrant ships meant disease spread readily on the cross-Atlantic voyage, and ships awaiting clearance in the harbour dumped their latrines in the bay. Most Hamiltonians got their drinking water from the bay, where the waste of the sick and dying had been discarded. It's estimated that eighteen percent of the city's population died of cholera in 1832. They were buried in a mass grave on Burlington Heights. By the time of the second major epidemic in 1854, contagion was better understood. Plans were put in place to build the water treatment plant on Woodward Avenue so that, by the 1860s, Hamiltonians had clean water from Lake Ontario, uncontaminated by the sewage in Hamilton Harbour.

When you follow water, you soon realize that it's not as humble and retiring as you first assumed. We dump our waste into its embrace and it doesn't seem to protest, meekly carting it around the corner and out of view. But later on, as we are loading loved ones into a mass grave, we wish we had been more attentive to its shy voice.

Years after Hamilton Harbour was declared unfit for swimming or fishing, the city began to separate stormwater runoff pipes from sewage pipes in the new parts of the city (mostly above the escarpment). Now a rainstorm would no longer send water into the same pipes where sewage flows. But it would be much too expensive to build a whole new second drainage system below the escarpment, in the old parts of the city. So, over the past five or ten years, the city has come up with a solution: building and burying huge CSO (combined sewage overflow) storage tanks.

From the map on the city's website, I count nine spots where these massive underground reservoirs the size of hockey arenas have been installed in low-lying ground around the lower city. The CSO tank buried where King and Main Streets cross Highway 403 has a capacity of seventy-five thousand cubic metres of combined storm- and sewer water. Not inches or litres – metres! That is a *lot* of water. The underground tank is so large that people play Sunday afternoon cricket games on the grassy surface that has been laid over it. The city website says that six of these CSO tanks hold the equivalent of one thousand Olympic-sized swimming pools. The idea behind these tanks is to divert overflow during thunderstorms into these enormous steel caverns and hold it there until drier days, when it can be pumped through the regular sewer system for treatment at the Woodward plant. The system of CSO tanks doesn't mean no sewer water will ever again be released into the watershed because, despite their enormous size, together they have the capacity to contain a twenty-five-millilitre rain (about an inch) across the city. That's a lot of rain, but if we get more than that, the excess still has to be flushed into the creeks and streams. In 2014, after the tanks were installed, the RBG recorded twenty million litres of contaminated water still being released over that year into the watershed that ends up in Cootes Paradise. That's the equivalent of eight Olympic swimming pools, but it's a hundred times less than the twenty billion litres that used to go into Cootes every year before the CSO tanks were installed.

A couple of years ago, the city buried one of these hockey arenas at the upper end of the university's parking lots, in the valley below our place. The mammoth track hoes digging down into the earth and filling the backs of the endless line of diesel-snorting dump trucks gave me the impression we were living on the edge of an open-pit mine. The crater they dug in the ground seemed the size of a whole neighbourhood. It must have taken about six months before they closed the moonscape back in. Today all you see is a little pumphouse, quaint as a goatherd's cottage, perched tidily on the graded earth of the valley floor just twenty or thirty metres from Ancaster Creek.

When our house was first built in 1949, the water from our roof would have trickled down into the ground and back out in the rills below our yard, and from there into the RBG wetlands below, where sediment settled among the reeds and bulrushes before the clean water from the marsh seeped into the creek. That's what marshes do: filter water. Then, after the university built its parking lots in the 1960s, the marsh could no longer do its work. Water was collected in runoff pipes, mixed with god-knows-what from sewer lines and flushed into the man-made creek. I remember walking along Ancaster Creek in 2008 during spring runoff with my nostrils clenched against the stench rising from the rank water. That's not supposed to happen anymore.

I wonder if any of our roof rain reaches Ancaster Creek these days. Perhaps some of it does – that is, if it comes out in those rills drained off under the parking lots and directly into Ancaster

Creek. Otherwise, it's fed into the CSO tank. The good thing is that less-corrupted water runs straight into the creek and Cootes Paradise. Over the past couple of years, Tys Theysmeyer, Head of Natural Lands at the RBG, and his team have been planting cat-tails, wild rice, water lilies and other indigenous water-filtering plants at the west end of the marsh, and they say it's working. With less junk flowing in from the watershed and all that filtra-tion, he says there are days where you can actually see the shallow bottom. For the first time in fifty years, a pair of bald eagles returned to fledge a couple of chicks four years ago, a sign that the wetland is a lot healthier than it's been for half a century.

Water is mysterious. It leads you places you've never imagined. Like the echoing caverns of CSO tanks and giant sewer systems that some people explore like cave spelunkers.

I'm serious.

My hiking partner, John Terpstra, alerted me to the under-city daredevils of www.vanishingpoint.ca, a website for trespassers who climb into the underground pipes and culverts under our city and post anonymous photos of their adventures. The pictures these ren-egades have taken inside storm sewers and culverts, where creeks have been buried under factories and highways, show underground passages twice as tall as a human. People actually do this. They want to know. They climb down and nose about the pipes and cavities where cities hide unwanted water. They take photographs of themselves in places that make you feel like you're looking at the nineteenth-century Paris sewers of *Les Misérables*.

I'd be nervous down in those tunnels. Once, John and I were out tracking Chedoke Creek, just one valley east of here. We scrambled down to the barred entrances of the culverts that bury the creek under Highway 403. We placed our hands on the rusty iron bars, leaned into the damp darkness and peered at the oil-slicked water below.

"How deep do you think it is?" I asked.

"Hard to tell," John said. "Doesn't make me want to be one of those Vanishing Point spelunkers. Who knows when an ocean of water is going to be flushed down a system like this? You'd need more than hip waders for a moment like that."

John and I keep our water tracking to the surface – aside from wading up channelized creeks or under highway bridges, and maybe an exploratory auger hole or two. We're content with guessing what's going on underground and living our lives for a few more years.

ULTIMATELY, HAMILTON IS HERE because of water. The Attawa-ndaron, and the Princess Point people before them, settled here because Cootes Paradise was the Dish with One Spoon, with its abundance of berries, wild rice, waterfowl and game. With this being the Head-of-the-Lake, it was also a crossroads. Travellers had to leave the open water and look for the easiest route up the escarpment. From here, westward or southward, they would have to follow the creeks feeding into Cootes. Whichever one they chose would require a portage when they reached the inevitable waterfall at the lip of the escarpment.

Ancaster Creek drops from two hundred fifty metres at its source above the lip to eighty metres above sea level below our place, where it merges with Spencer Creek. That's one hundred seventy metres' difference between here and the town of Ancaster, six kilometres from this backyard. This means it's a bigger drop between Ancaster on top of the escarpment and our house below it, than it is from Lake Ontario all the way down the St. Lawrence River to the Atlantic Ocean! Basically, this theatrical drop is part of the same escarpment formation that brings folks from all over the world to visit Niagara Falls an hour's drive east of here.

This busy, dramatic place was a junction for both water and foot travel. People in canoes would have followed the marsh and creeks up this valley once they left the lake. Bob Henderson, a friend of mine who used to teach at McMaster, is passionate about historical travel and geography. He spends any time he can tracking the travels of early explorers and fur traders by canoe, foot and – when he needs to – airplane. Bob thinks that one of the portages from Lake Ontario likely followed either Sulphur Creek or Ancaster Creek. Travellers would have been aiming to meet the old Mohawk path that rimmed the escarpment around the lake. The maps that exist from the 1670s and 1680s aren't detailed enough to pinpoint where people like La Salle or Galinée climbed up. Bob thinks the village where those first Frenchmen stayed a night or two in the Attawandaron village of Tinawatawa could have been at the intersection of what's now Wilson and Rousseaux Streets on the edge of Ancaster town – or thereabouts. If he's right, this would make Ancaster Creek, before it joins Spencer Creek just upstream from McMaster University's parking lot M, what he calls "the end of navigation."

That's somewhere upstream from where mountains of earth were trucked away and the CSO tank is now buried.

Other local rock and river readers, including John, have suggested different paths up the escarpment. The two of us once hiked up an abandoned section of Filman Road, a little east of Tiffany Falls, to see if its ascent would make sense as an old portage route. We tracked along a seasonal creek bed, running in spring and dry in summer, under one-hundred-foot maples and oaks. The creek bed's fold ascended around mossy boulders and over gravel ledges to the cut in the escarpment where Highway 403 bursts onto the tableland above. It seemed to us a likely possibility. Archaeologists have found evidence of substantial Indigenous habitation right there, where the 403 circles the big box stores of Meadowlands Power Centre. So the merchants of Meadowlands have ancient forebears in the traders who carried furs, wampum beads, flint rocks or copper ingots in their packs to and from their canoes below. Whichever water route is the right one, then, Ancaster Creek valley would have been the staging area from the marsh to the portage.

When the water was high in the spring, canoe parties would have paddled upstream from the reeds of Cootes Paradise, loud with red-winged blackbirds, under the willows along Spencer Creek to where Ancaster Creek branches off just below the parking lots. They would have taken the Ancaster Creek branch, and at some point they'd have had to carry their cargo up the most gradual grade they could find to the top of the escarpment to avoid Sherman Falls, Tiffany Falls or Canterbury Falls, each on a different branch of the creek system. Later in the year, with water too shallow to paddle very far up Ancaster Creek, they would have had to pull the canoes out of the water and onto the mud somewhere in the flats of the valley below our house.

It's likely that this valley was a parking lot for canoes long before it became a parking lot for cars.

Settlers, too, came here because of water. At first, as with La Salle, Galinée and the others, they came because of the water route. But later, they set up shop here – as in workshops – because of the same waterfalls in Ancaster and Dundas that required travellers to detour. The newcomers who arrived from New York and Pennsylvania after the Revolutionary War saw potential power generators in the local waterfalls. They built dozens of mills around Spencer and Ancaster creeks: gristmills, sawmills, paper mills, linseed oil mills, cotton and wool carding mills, tanneries, foundries, garden tool factories, distilleries and eventually, by the end of the nineteenth century, generators of electricity.

The water took on new roles.

During this period, it became a resource. Rowdy, falling water was used to transform nature's elements – trees, grain seeds, sheep's wool – into products such as four-by-fours, bread and clothes. The town of Dundas Mills grew into a bustling worksite where flour bags, garden rakes and wool sweaters were stacked onto flat-bottomed barges and floated out through Cootes Paradise, to ships waiting in Hamilton Harbour.

To get there, mill owners in the region cut a channel deep enough for ships through the Beach Strip that divided Lake Ontario from what we today call Hamilton Harbour, then known as Burlington Bay – the name officially changed in 1919. They then dug a second canal through the Iroquois Bar and Cootes Paradise to Dundas Mills. Intrepid dredging brought the Great Lakes and the St. Lawrence within their reach.

This brief moment of glory didn't last long. Soon water changes roles again, and steam shouldered out waterfalls as a main source of power. Coal-fired locomotives and steamships

boosted Hamilton Harbour ahead of Dundas Mills as commercial front-runner at the Head-of-the-Lake. Steam was portable
– you could take it with you and, in turn, it could take you and
your commodities, too. There's a reason why we say "steaming
ahead," with its echoes of aggressive industrial swagger. Sir Allan MacNab, for example, had been president of the Desjardins
Canal Company, promoting sluggish barge transport to sailing
ships in the Harbour before 1834. But silt kept filling up the
canal through Cootes Paradise, and he soon turned his energies to railways, becoming chief promoter and president of the
Hamilton and Port Dover Railway and a director of the Great
Western Railway. He benefited immediately from these involve-
ments, selling large blocks of his Hamilton lands to railway
developments in 1835 and 1837. He served as president of the
Great Western Railway from 1845 to 1849 and as chair of the
railway committee for the Upper Canada Legislative Assembly
seven times between 1848 and 1857, blatantly using his political
position to expand his financial holdings. He had purchased the
Beasley property from J.S. Cartwright on the Iroquois Bar back
in 1832 and built his ostentatious seventy-two-room manor
house there, which he called Dundurn Castle. Then the Great
Western Railway ran a rail line into town along the slim margin
of land beside the bay and below his windows, where he could
keep an eye on his investments – and collect a hefty payment
for the margin of land he sold to the company. He could smell
the coal smoke turning water into cash from his front lawn.
No wonder he bragged, deep in his cups, to a friend one day in
1851, "All my politics are railroads." That was the year he sold
the waterfront to his own company.

MacNab's rail service along the lakeshore helped Hamilton shoulder its way into its twentieth-century role as Steel Town, and the mills of Dundas fell increasingly silent as water power was replaced by steam; so much so that the mills eventually dropped off of the town's name. Looking back, we might consider Dundas's decline as its salvation, because it never became as extensively industrialized as Hamilton did, and today remains a quaint town hidden in a green valley.

The Hamilton railway needed iron and steel to build locomotives, railcars and ties. What better place to build smelters than by a deep harbour where heavy lakers could unload ore from the continent's largest iron mines, shipping from the ports of Marquette and Escanaba in Michigan's northern peninsula? In turn, the railways and ships could send steel and iron products to market throughout the growing industrial hub of the Great Lakes in both the USA and Canada. So, between the 1820s and 1920s, the little family-run mills on Spencer and Ancaster Creeks fell into disrepair as huge, coke-fired, corporate-run smelters pushed into the sky along the harbour's south shore. The swagger of the city came to be measured by the number of smokestacks and the size of the black plumes lifted into the sky, as compared to its competitors in Buffalo, Erie, Detroit and Pittsburgh. For the first seventy years of the twentieth century, steel smelting and the manufacture of everything from automobiles to elevators was what made Hamilton Hamilton.

All this activity depended on water – not only on the power of the creeks and the capacity of the harbour, but also on Hamilton's abundant supplies of good, fresh water piped into the city from outside the polluted harbour. Cholera had taught everybody a lesson, and the city almost bankrupted itself building a grand system of pumps and pipes that could bring plenty of clean water right downtown. The big fountain in Gore Park, the city's triangular central "square," that ran water day and night, became a proud sign of Hamilton's gumption. The steel mills needed power to create heat and plenty of water to cool it afterwards, and the combination of the hydroelectricity generated from water tumbling off the Niagara Escarpment and abundant water in Lake Ontario filled these needs precisely.

Still, worries recurred about water quality at the Head-of-the-Lake. As far back as the 1870s, when creeks running into the bay ran thick with city waste, the city tried to smother the contagion by dumping infill into the inlets along the south shore of the bay. The steel mills expanded their buildings on the new dry ground. But the problem could not simply be buried. Swimmers climbed out of the bay in 1925 coated in oil, and by 1946, Hamilton's health officer had shut down the north shore bathing areas and change rooms because of polluted water. These popular swimming areas have never reopened.

THAT'S THE PROBLEM WITH the humility of water. It accepts whatever is dumped into it and then hides it from view. For a while.

The death of Lake Erie in the 1960s, just an hour's drive south of Hamilton, across the Niagara Peninsula, finally got people's attention. As Mark Sproule-Jones puts it, Lake Erie showed signs of anoxia as early as 1953, and by the 1960s, newspapers had pronounced the lake dead. It suffered from human-fed eutrophication. In this process, phosphates leaching from fertilized farm fields fed algae blooms of such scale that in the summer months there was little oxygen left in Erie for fish or other plants. Because the Great Lakes make up about twenty percent of the world's fresh water and are home to thirty-three million people who live around them in the industrial gut of the United States and Canada, it's not hard to understand why people grew anxious. If Erie was dead, what would happen to the other lakes, and to the people who depended on them?

Public outcry provoked a response. In 1967, the federal government launched the Canadian Centre for Inland Waters to study water quality in Hamilton Harbour. Five years later, the Great Lakes Water Quality Agreement was signed by the USA and Canada, and its International Joint Commission registered forty-three "major areas of concern" across the Great Lakes system. Hamilton Harbour was high on the list.

Students in hip waders splashed up the creeks. Water samples were captured in test tubes. Scientists peered through microscopes. Reports were written. Not only was the harbour a quarter smaller than it had been before the reeking inlets were filled in back at the turn of the twentieth century, but one-quarter of the wetlands that surrounded it were now dead and gone, too. Remedial action plans were generated.

Even though the steel industry here has dropped off significantly over the past twenty years, Hamilton Harbour is still one of the busiest commercial ports on the Great Lakes, docking over a thousand vessels a year. The coke ovens at U.S. Steel have been "hot idled," and workers laid off in droves. A lot of work has been done to improve water quality during this period of massive slowdown in steel. However, as recently as 2007, Sproule-Jones wrote there were still seven industrial and four municipal pipes pouring twenty-seven billion gallons of liquid waste into the bay. At the time, this waste added up to forty percent of the harbour's total volume. Converted to litres, this is over ninety billion, making the twenty billion litres diverted from Cootes Paradise by the CSO tank system miniscule by comparison. Despite the reduction of steel production and the diversion of waste water since 2007, the pollutants don't just disappear. The bay still contains toxic levels of phosphorus, ammonia, heavy metals, polychlorinated biphenyl (PCB) and polycyclic aromatic hydrocarbons (PAHs), also known as coal tar.

The most notorious pile of corruption in the bay is known as Randle Reef, named after Harvey T. Randle, the veteran Hamilton Harbour Commission marine pilot who was dumbfounded when, in 1964, the hull of his boat ground up against something underwater in an area where he had navigated freely for years. The incident happened on a natural shoal just west of one of the docks at Stelco, the largest of the steel manufacturers in Hamilton (now owned, and declared bankrupt, by U.S. Steel). It was soon obvious that the shoal was collecting industrial pollutants, but the inevitable finger pointing among Stelco, other industries on Sherman Inlet and government regulators obscured and delayed any reliable investigation, let alone solid commitments to remediation.

It took twenty years before scientists from Environment Canada were able to complete a study that no one could dispute. The 1988 study described a huge pile of coal tar compounds and metals laced with extreme levels of PCBs, PAHs, dioxins, furans and organochlorines. This toxic dump is enormous. An article in *Hamilton Magazine* cites its size as about that of 120 football fields, covering sixty hectares. With over a million tonnes of polluted sediment needing to be cleaned up, that makes it five times the size of the two hundred thousand tonnes of the notorious tar ponds in Sydney, Nova Scotia. This underwater mountain of oily, oozing sludge lies right near the Stelco pier, where ship propellers stir up a current around Randle Reef, spreading its effluents each time one of them pulls into dock.

Stelco claimed to know nothing about Randle Reef, and subsequent reports have indicated that the contamination began long before Stelco built its pier there. The Ontario Ministry of the Environment certified that in 1984 a spill from the company had been properly dredged and removed. And the Hamilton Port Authority assured the public that it had conducted shipping lane dredging in the late 1980s, but the paperwork on this operation somehow went missing. If there are reasons not to see them, point sources can be extremely elusive. Some cleanup workers later reported that the dredged toxins were transported to an industrial landfill near Sarnia, Ontario, and classified as hazardous waste. But whatever the Ministry of the Environment and the Port Authority said, Randle Reef is still there.

People haven't let government and business off the hook. After the head-in-the-sand collusions of government and industry had basically done nothing, a group of concerned Hamiltonians began organizing the Bay Area Restoration Council (BARC) in 1985. Their idea was to widen input and bring together environmental groups, the federal and provincial Ministries of the Environment, industry leaders and researchers from McMaster

University, as well as the Canada Centre for Inland Waters, to look into possible solutions. BARC's studies showed that Randle Reef was much bigger than the initial estimates suggested. In the 1980s, official reports claimed the reef consisted of twenty thousand cubic metres of coal tar; however, the figure released at the annual BARC community workshop I attended in September 2011 was 630,000 cubic metres of contaminated sediment – that's about a million tonnes, more than thirty times the original estimates.

At the 2011 workshop, environmental engineers summarized different solutions that had been proposed and rejected over the last thirty-odd years. Dredging up the pile could stir up the toxins and spread them even more widely throughout the bay. And dredging then raised the problem of transportation, with thousands of trucks carrying carcinogenic material through the city. Furthermore, where could the toxic glue be placed, once it had been dug up? Some speculated that burning it in one of the steel plant's many-thousand-degree ovens might dispense with the problem; some noted, however, that burning could pump the toxins into the air. Others suggested bio-cleanup, but the companies who claimed their micro-organic bacteria could eat away the deadly sludge had no record of cleaning up a mess this large.

Over a decade of study and debate later, the BARC-brokered coalition finally decided that the best solution is to cap Randle Reef in a two-ply steel-walled, 7.5 hectare "Engineered Containment Facility." Because ship propellers over the years have spread contaminated silt across the bay floor, huge suction systems will be used to vacuum up the toxic spread and pour it into this massive steel bin. Eventually, once all the contaminated sediment has been collected, it will be capped, and the surface of the cap could be used as a green-topped pier or storage facility. This $138 million project is supposed to take almost a decade to complete.

I've kept an eye on the paper since that workshop in 2011, and I see that the federal, provincial and city governments have come up with their contributions for this complex undertaking. According to the *Hamilton Spectator*, even U.S. Steel is supposed to be contributing. It's five years later, and only this past summer did they finally begin pounding the steel containment walls into the harbour floor.

SO WATER IS HUMBLE, but in a muscle-bound way. On one hand, it shrinks and shies away. It meekly takes whatever we toss into it, hides it and slips off out of sight. But then it returns where and when we don't expect it. And when it does, look out.

Consider Walkerton, Ontario, a town of five thousand people one hundred fifty kilometres from here. In the year 2000, run-off from a four-day rain in May surged across farm fields and into the town's drinking water. The shallowest of the town's wells was contaminated with E. coli, and two thousand three hundred townsfolk got sick, with blood in their diarrhea and intense stomach pains. Seven people died. A public inquiry found that manure spread on farmland near the well had swept into the water. In this case, they could put their finger on the point source.

The Ontario government of the day had surged into power with what it called a "common sense revolution" that emphasized austerity measures and efficiency by getting rid of big government and creating a lean civil service. With the surprising exception of the government of Justin Trudeau, elected in 2015, this line of thinking seems to be everywhere in politics these days: cut taxes, cut public spending, create as poor a civil service as you can. But then, when something like Walkerton happens, people suddenly complain: "Where are the water quality inspectors? Why didn't they enforce regulations?" Real common sense would say you pay for what you get. According to Carolyn Johns, editor of the book *Canadian Water Politics*, the Ontario government under Premier Mike Harris cut funding to the Ministry of the Environment (MOE) by three-quarters over ten years, which left the MOE with half the employees it used to have. This reduction left very few people to carry out inspections.

Who watches the watchmen? And who manages the managers?

Maybe the water itself. Maybe water keeps us honest. In the Walkerton case, the point source of the contamination was traced to a specific well. But who traces the human point source? Two men in the local water utility took the fall for not raising the alert about E. coli in the water, but the responsibility for properly staffing the utility evaporated in the upper echelons.

Water has a way of eluding management, as John and I discovered on a hike up the Chedoke Radial Trail that climbs the escarpment overlooking Highway 403. We were not far from the vista where Marks and Mathelena Binkley stood gazing over the Dish With One Spoon and decided to live out their lives here. Beside us on the cliff wall, Princess Falls splattered over the lip. The water was funnelled under the path we were standing on and down a huge concrete chute hanging on the cliff face, then into a square culvert under the highway below. But here's the thing: no water was running into the culvert. Not a drop.

We leaned over the edge to see better. The massive chute descending below us was cracked and humped on its way down the escarpment drop. And the creek giggled quietly into one of these cracks before vanishing into the limestone jumble at the bottom.

We both began to laugh. Soon, I had my hands on my knees, trying to catch my breath.

"Why is it so funny?" I gasped.

"I don't know!" John said, gulping for air. "I feel bad for the engineers. Shouldn't we mourn all that human effort? The water just bypasses the whole thing."

Nonetheless, it's understandable, or predictable at any rate, that municipalities and governments would try to manage water. Their whole reason for being is about managing all kinds of things, hopefully on behalf of their citizens. It's understandable that engineers and planners talk about managing water. It's in their job description. However, you can see how much the language of management, control and restraint economics has soaked our collective brains when you hear environmentalists also using this kind of talk.

I was looking recently at a 2010 brochure put out by the Ontario Water Conservation Alliance called *One Water: Supporting Watershed Management and Green Infrastructure in Ontario Policy*. I'm inclined to think of the people who publish brochures like this as being friends of willowed creek valleys like the one in which I live. I appreciate them for trying to remind us all that the water we depend on isn't just limpid lakes and crystal-clear rivers in a postcard wilderness. It's right here, in the city we live in, and, as their title says, it's all one water: from the rills whispering out of the slope above the university parking lots to the huge CSO tanks under our feet, not to mention the slow-releasing cancer of Randle Reef. So I tend to think that the folks who wrote this and I are playing on the same team.

But I'm troubled by their language.

They talk about managing water rather than people, and they latch desperately onto the language of budgets and accounting. Presumably, that's the only way to get the public's ear. Their brochure calls readers' attention to the "natural capital" of the Credit River just down the road in Mississauga. They suggest that this river alone provides "services" worth more than $371 million each year to area residents, including water supply and filtration. And they calculate that services provided by this one watershed alone save taxpayers "$100.5 million in water supply costs" every year, since the municipality doesn't have to pump water from Lake Ontario.

You can see the logic: tell people they should care about what happens to the water in their neighbourhood because it's money in the bank. Fine upstanding supporters of the common sense revolution will see that nature pays you back. "Canada has a large freshwater 'bank account,'" writes David Schindler, winner of the first Stockholm Water Prize in 1991, "the interest rate is very low.... It is the interest we have to use [rather than the principal] if we want to sustain our water capital."

Where are we if we can only value clean water as a service, a commodity, as money in the bank? And what happens if the accounts don't add up? What if Ancaster Creek, being so much smaller than the Credit River, is only worth a few thousand bucks? How will its credits stand up against its debits when someone, promising jobs and a boost to the economy, wants to build a multi-million dollar highway or run a crude oil pipeline along its path?

A friend of mine, Max Haiven, calls this wallet-thinking the financialization of the imagination. It shoehorns a living network of interdependent, breathing beings into accountants' ledgers. If we can't see what links the water in our drinking glass to shade trees and fresh air and black soil and our own happiness; if we can't see this oneness as straight-up beautiful, not for us or our wallets, but for itself, then we really are, quite literally, up shit creek.

A group of McMaster scientists, engineers and ecologists don't want to think about water in terms of money. Rather than thinking of the value of Ancaster Creek valley in terms of the number of parking spots it provides, they have begun a campaign with the university to try to manage the people and not the water.

When the city dug up the west end of the parking lots for that huge CSO tank, it had arranged to compensate the university for the costs of repaving the lot after the job was done. It took a couple of years to tender the job to a paving company. That pause in paving created a pause for thought. It showed that the university had plenty of parking to go around. So the McMaster group asked, why repave? Didn't the two years show we don't need to asphalt the whole valley? This gap in time created a chance to see what happens when a compromised watershed has a chance to restore itself. So why don't we rename the area the McMarsh Living Lab and make it a site where groups of students and researchers from different fields can study what happens when a disturbed wetland is allowed to return to its own rhythms and patterns?

To do this, the group received a small grant to install ground-water and stream stage wells in order to collect baseline data on underground flow paths. Once they have figured out what's happening with the water system – after the area has been capped in asphalt for forty years and then turned into a moonscape when the CSO tank was buried – the group can watch what happens as the groundwater begins again to find its own patterns. At the McMarsh Living Lab, the group can also collect information on the diversity of bird, animal and plant species and how they might change as the water reasserts itself unhindered.

While they were at it, the McMarsh group reminded the university that, according to its own regulations, the remaining parking lots don't conform to the thirty-metre buffer that is supposed to separate the asphalt from the creek. Added to this, the non-point source rills that emerge from the slope all along this side of the valley appear to be springs. And if they are, the whole parking lot scheme in this flood plain needs serious reconsideration, given the importance of this part of the valley to the overall health of the Ancaster and Spencer Creek watershed.

These activities look like water management – boring holes for test wells, checking water levels, making checklists for birds and plants, digging back the asphalt from the buffer zone and replacing it with soil.

But in truth they are really people management. The group is asking tough questions: Why did we pave a water-cleaning wetland in the first place? Do more parking lots mean a bigger university, and is a bigger university intrinsically a better thing? Basically, the group is trying to get people to think differently, to limit our own reach, to dam our self-destructive ambitions.

These university teachers and students remind us all that the water sinking into this slope and hiding from our view feeds us. We need the willows, cattails, algae, and even weed trees like alder and buckthorn in order to live and breathe. Water doesn't need managing. We do.

As Randy Kaye, one of the instigators of the McMarsh project, put it, maybe this time we can restore paradise and dig up a parking lot.

WE HUMANS MIGHT HAVE come here for the water, but we are also leery of it. We want to get close, maybe have a nice view of a seashore or live on a lake framed by trees, but we don't want to be too close, because water floods basements, rots foundations, warps floorboards. Except for surges and tsunamis, it does its damage silently, out of sight in the dark. For this reason, places like Ancaster Creek valley, hemmed in by new housing subdivisions on its upper end, by a large golf course in its middle section and by university parking lots below the escarpment, tend to escape the city. This valley interrupts the built city with a wide tract of unlooked-for marshy ground treed with willows, ash and black walnut. I had lived on its lip for fifteen years but hadn't realized, until I got curious about following water, that this huge, green, sap-scented world existed, right beside my house.

Following water opens the land to you, and it also opens you to the land. Mostly, we humans don't notice. We follow the road or the sidewalk, which shows us the front side, the face, the fronts of stores and homes. The faces of many homes are dominated by big double garage doors, a larger welcome for travellers on four tires than those on two legs. The high street, as it's known in Britain, is made for seeing and being seen. From one street to the next you see the same things – the same windows, doors, awnings, taxis and cars and buses, newsstands, people in suits and leather shoes, jeans and T-shirts. Sometimes you see bits of green – perfectly spaced trees, perfectly trimmed hedges, perfectly clipped lawns on well-kept streets – or raggedy patches of goldenrod edging old parking lots, with crab grass poking through cracks in the asphalt of forgotten ones. Each city does it differently, but the overall geometry remains the same.

Water, however, rarely shows up on the high street. It is always looking for haven somewhere low, out of sight, along a ditch of leaves and fast-food containers, through a dented culvert and down again into a runoff behind a parkade. It escapes to the wastelands in the city's backside. Because it cuts the ground and follows the slice, deepening as it goes, it's the enemy of the high street. It flees from roads, sidewalks, parking lots, shopping malls. For the built world, it's a problem, a real nuisance. The sinks, ravines, marshes, ditches and valleys it loves become the useless, abandoned parts of urban development. You can't build there because the ground of the flood plain is rough and soggy, the asphalt bucks and sags.

When you follow water, you see what the city has left behind, both its junk and what it couldn't colonize. You encounter land, spaces and places that most urban people do not know. Ancaster Creek makes a whole, breathing world. Another place, another time, hidden in plain sight.

Among our various itineraries, John and I set out a few years ago to explore the Ancaster Creek watershed in a series of walks from autumn right through winter and into spring. We hiked upstream from the lower creek, where the runoff pipes emerge from under the university parking lots, just above the spot where Ancaster Creek empties into Spencer. We ran our fingers along the teeth marks on the dozen or so saplings that had been felled by beavers. We clumped through the football field of mud around the pumphouse, freshly landscaped on top of the underground CSO tank. We pushed through waist-high goldenrod and rose bush brambles upstream from the pumphouse. As we walked, we tried to keep track of the ditches and cuts in the earth that drained rivulets and rills into the creek.

Upstream from the seven-foot-tall culvert that pours the creek under Osler Drive, we were startled to encounter a wide-open valley where the creek snakes in oxbow curves through a large flood plain, guarded by willows and Manitoba maples. This is what the whole valley must have looked like before the university paved the lower end near our place, bulldozed the original meandering path of the creek and forced it into its present-day channel on the west side of the parking lots. This late in the fall, most of the reeds and goldenrod had browned off and weren't much of an obstacle, especially when we followed the deer trails along the creek's lazy path.

Down there on the flats, the creek is slow moving, brown with soil. Silent. Time seems to meander. The diesel fumes from trucks on Wilson Street and Osler Drive don't drift this far. Television and cell phone signals could be swirling all around us, but we might as well be living in the pre-electric age. The dirt banks themselves, eaten into oxbows, were laid down in the first place by sediment. The water slurps up sand and loam, lays it elsewhere, consumes it again. And the marsh down at Cootes Paradise archives it all – the silt, PCBs, cracked water bottles, car tires, willow branches, last year's oak leaves. Then the Stewards of Cootes, who organize volunteer teams to clean up creeks and shorelines throughout the watershed, sieve the human bric-a-brac from its memory.

A kilometre or so above the marshy wetland and closer to the escarpment cliffs, the creek falls more quickly between banks anchored by ash, maple, oak, fir, beech, an odd sycamore and willows everywhere. Here, you could imagine you were in a wilderness park, somewhere up north maybe, or hiking in the mountains. The air feels cooler and the water rushes clear over rocks rounded by thousands of years of water running over them. This far upstream, the water gurgles and sings. Time grows lively in these uplands. The air smells sprightly and vigorous. But John and I don't feel busier or more hurried in this active zone. We're just as happy to stop and look here as we were in the bottomlands. In fact, we like this section more. It's got more going on, more variety than the lower parts of the creek. The water's got less silt in it; it looks cleaner, fresher. We can see the bottom, trace the details of red willow roots, the green streamers of underwater grass pointing downstream. The energy of this part of the creek makes it seem younger.

John picks up a length of birch bark and lobs it in, to watch it sail around the corner. Then he tosses in a broken branch.

"Hey!" I say. "Doesn't the creek have enough junk in it already?"

"What?" He grins. "You didn't have a childhood?"

If I lift my gaze, from the emerald of the bank moss and the dark leaves on the trees to the rim of the valley, I can glimpse here and there the tops of apartment high-rises along Wilson Street or, to the west, the 1960s ranch-style homes clinging to the valley edge along Little John Road in Dundas. And right here, if the water made no sound, I would hear city bus brakes squealing up to stops on Wilson. It's a wonder that with all these roads and their attendant storm sewers still shunting runoff and warm water into this valley, Ancaster Creek still qualifies as a cold-water creek. Its temperatures are still low enough to sustain fish species like rainbow and fantail darter, brassy minnow and three kinds of dace – finescale, pearl and northern redbelly. People have even spotted rainbow trout and American brook lamprey in this creek. Left to itself, water's need for a hideaway has created a kind of eco-preserve that runs pretty much unnoticed under Main Street.

Literally.

Here, birds and animals on the endangered list, such as prothonotary warblers, Acadian flycatchers and eastern milk snakes, plus endangered plants like red mulberries and American chestnuts still survive alongside species that the Conservation Authority calls "threatened," like Blanding's turtles, Jefferson salamanders, least bitterns and white wood asters. Here and there, a toppled willow skims surface detritus as the creek glides silent underneath. Its broken arms pick up old tires, rusted grocery carts and yellowed plastic water bottles flushed downstream by heavy rains.

According to the *Ancaster Creek Subwatershed Stewardship Action Plan*, 365 people live in each square kilometre of this watershed. Even though Dundas's mills are long gone, there's still a lot of industry spread along this system, and the amount of "impervious surfacing" – parking lots and roads that leak petro-chemicals from asphalt into the water table – is far above limits for healthy stream systems.

Nonetheless, this eco-preserve known as Ancaster Creek valley perseveres.

During the winter, John and I hiked up sections of the creek where the ice was thick, following tracks of white-tailed deer. The deer didn't seem to worry about breaking through the ice. We could see where their pointy hooves had punched down into the cold water below. Their breakthroughs showed us where to make a wide detour on shoreline, rocks or deadfalls. We came across part of a deer's skull and much of the vertebrae – signs of poach-ers, perhaps, and city coyotes. I know there are a lot of deer: I once counted twenty-two whitetails in this valley in two short hours one Sunday afternoon.

In late spring, John and I teetered across the creek on one of the deadfall willows and stepped into a six-acre parkland of waist-high purple rocket, their flowers waving like a white and purple crop in the filtered light of black walnuts towering over-head. When we rounded another oxbow curve, we come upon an acre of yellow flag irises nodding in the breeze. The air was sweet with pollen, loud with bees.

Sometimes, when I think of our culture's disregard for these lives around us, I can hardly believe that this valley is here. That it is *still* here. That, for all the crowding and disrespect, nature is never spent.

"Who are we?" asks the poet Rita Wong in *undercurrent*, her book tracking water's surging, retiring ways. "We are the beings

who need clean water ... we are the thunderstorms that precipi-
tate when too much has been repressed, the weeds that refuse to
stop, the coyotes, the grandmothers, the yet unborn." We are – no
matter what clan or species or mineral – citizens of this watershed, subjects of its interconnected, many-branched kingdom.

Broken Pine

WE LIVE IN THE shelter of a broken pine. This tree stands, stunted, in the northwest corner of the yard. Like all of us here at the Head-of-the-Lake, it's had its misadventures.

Six years before we moved into this house, a windstorm splintered the tree's spine twenty-five feet up. Given how tall and top heavy these trees get, it's a wonder their spines don't break off all the time. The biologist David George Haskell says that wood fibre is made of millions of tiny coils, all layered over each other and angled in different directions, which is why living wood is so springy. He quotes the Taoist poet Lao Tzu: "Grass and trees are pliant and fragile when living, but dried and shriveled when dead. Thus the hard and strong are the comrades of death; the supple and the weak are the comrades of life." Green wood survives storms by keeping limber. Among the trees around here, you soon realize that white pines are even more extreme than the Tao suggests, because it's true that they bend, but they also break. They break easily. Their branches and trunks sway in the wind, but when breeze becomes gale, they snap right off. After a big windstorm, I always go out into the tangy air and gather up the pine boughs that litter the yard. There might also be one or two sprigs of softwood maple on the grass, but never any oak branches. Among the trees, white pines survive by giving way, by bending easily and, if that's not enough, breaking.

The pines in our yard are mostly sheltered from superstrong winds by the escarpment. But on rare occasions, the wind reverses its usual westerly origin and snarls in off Lake Ontario from the east, and then we're in for a storm. When one such storm splintered the top of this tree, Mrs. Forbes, who would have been in her mid-eighties at the time, had the jagged break sawn off smooth above one of those hubs where the branches shoot out from the trunk like the legs of starfish.

White pines branch regularly. You could picture them as one of those staircases you see in ships or fire halls, but instead of spiralling around a central spar, their steps climb to the heavens, dividing off in evenly spaced rungs that spread out from the trunk like spokes in a wagon wheel. A ladder with one stout central leg. Compared to the hardwoods that dominate this region's Carolinian forests, white pines grow quickly, leaping upward in search of light. They tend to grow straight up, soon towering high above most of the other trees in the woods – except the occasional oak or black walnut.

Our broken pine is not alone. It stands in the fringe of woods that slopes from our place down toward the university parking lots below. It's joined by a huge, two-hundred-year-old northern red oak, a dozen softwood maples, a couple of tall black walnuts, a mid-sized fir, a twisted basswood and five other white pines. Two of these pines tower – proud and unbroken – seventy and eighty feet into the sky at the top of the slope. My field guide to North American trees says white pines add a set of branches each year, and these two have about fifty rungs each – which makes sense, since the house was built in 1949 and these would have been planted soon after. At fifty, they already rival the height of the two-hundred-year-old oak.

The broken tree has the same girth as the two fifty-year-olds, so it's likely the same age. But it is, well, truncated: hardly a ship's ladder to heaven, more like a platform for a tree house. A friend once said we should put a lawn chair up there. We'd have a bird's-eye view of the Ancaster Creek valley below. With its crown lopped off, the starfish legs of its branches have curved awkwardly up into the bowl of air at the top, each branch hungry for light. The result is that the tree now looks like a cockeyed satellite dish, searching the skies for some kind of sign. Its scars are obvious, but it's not sick or starving; it's thriving actually, booming brokenly into the air.

A few years ago, I attended a ceremony where the hosts gave their guests white pine seedlings as gifts. An agreement was being signed between scholars and teachers at Six Nations Polytechnic on the reserve and McMaster University, where I work. The idea was to establish the Deyohahá:ge: Indigenous Knowledge Centre, where Iroquois knowledge, languages and culture would be revitalized through research and language study. At the ceremony, baby pines in plastic pots wrapped in cellophane and tied with bright green ribbons were handed to guests, so they could take them home and plant them in their yards.

White pine, known as ohnehta'kowa in the Mohawk language, is the Tree of Peace, and it stands at the heart of the Iroquois Confederacy, the governing body of the Hodinöhsö:ni' Longhouse.

"Trees capture the memory of the land and help define the cultural landscape," writes Rick Hill, Tuscarora scholar and artist, and senior project coordinator at Deyohahá:ge, in a McMaster Museum of Art exhibition brochure essay on "The Restorative Aesthetic of Greg Staats."

To the Hodinöhsö:ni', the white pine is the ohnehta'kowa, the tree of the long leaves or needles. They grow in clusters of five, the original number of nations who accepted the kayaneren'tsherakowa as their way of life. I've heard various Hodinöhsö:ni' people translate this word as "the great niceness," "the great warmth," and, most commonly, "the great law of peace." The founding of the Six Nations Confederacy dates back to the story of the Peacemaker. He was a Huron child born to a virgin mother somewhere near the present-day town of Belleville, on the north shore of Lake Ontario. Around a thousand years ago, the Peacemaker paddled across the lake in a canoe he'd carved from white stone and landed among peoples who were at war. The Finger Lakes region in what's now New York State was burning with distrust, murder and violence.

Peacemaker said it did not have to be this way. He taught everybody the three principles at the heart of the kayaneren'tsherakowa, the great law: Peace (healthy minds and bodies bring peace), Power (or strength in unity) and Righteousness (having a clear or good mind). Calm and quiet thinking, he said, could stop the fighting and bring peace. The Kanien'kehá:ka, or Mohawks, were first to accept Peacemaker's message, which gradually spread to the other four nations – the Oneida, Onondaga, Cayuga and Seneca – who lived in the Finger Lakes area. There's a lake named after each one of them, except the Mohawks, who lived farther east on what's today called the Hudson River. Together, the Peacemaker and leaders from these five nations worked out the principles for a confederation that would constitute the longhouse, after which they named themselves Hodinöhsö:ni', "they are building the house."

In an act that recalls the uprooting of the Tree of Lights in the Skyworld, Peacemaker is said to have lifted a towering white pine out of the ground, and the people threw their weapons into the hole where its roots used to be. The underground rivers then washed the armaments away.

"From now on," he said, "anyone can track the white roots of the pine from anywhere in the world's four directions if they want to find the way of peace." Thus, the symbol of onerahtase'ko:wa, the Great Tree of Peace, was derived from the tall tree of the five needles, ohnehta'kowa, which anyone could see any day growing throughout the region's woods.

The Tuscaroras tracked those roots of peace in the 1720s, when they fled from settler invasions in the south to join the Confederacy in what's now New York State. They became the sixth rafter in the Hodinöhsö:ni' Longhouse. Other smaller nations like the Tutelos and some Nanticokes added rafters, too, though they weren't added in the official numbering. So we don't talk about the Seven or Eight Nations, even though there were others that joined. To belong, all you had to do was see the good mind in the kayaneren'tsherakowa. The peace you found in the Great Law could become your heritage, a pillow in the land on which you could lay your head and rest.

Peacemaker placed Skadjí'nä, or Eagle, at the top of onerahtase'ko:wa. His powerful eyes would see any danger approaching and warn everybody.

I'VE NEVER SEEN AN eagle land on our sawed-off pine. Not even pass above it in the air.

Recently though, a pair has begun to turn grand circles in the sky above Cootes Paradise. Birders in this region are rejoicing at the return of eagles to the Head-of-the-Lake. Given the pollution in the waters of Hamilton Harbour and Cootes Paradise, bald eagles have abandoned this area for the past fifty years. Seeing them back in the air over our heads is a sign that the cleanup is starting to pay off.

It wasn't just Lake Erie that was declared dead in the 1970s. Cootes Paradise received the same coroner's report back then. Its water stank of heavy metals, PCBs and phosphorous-fed algae. Its plant life had been clear-cut by bottom-feeding *cyprinus carpio*, a carp introduced to the Great Lakes from Europe and Asia, so the marsh could no longer filter and clean the water that passed through. Studies of water birds at the Head-of-the-Lake showed that only twenty-nine percent of common terns' eggs were hatchable. When scientists tested the eggs to see what was wrong with them, they found organochlorine compounds like hexachlorobenzene, dichlorodiphenyldichloroethylene (DDE), dieldrin, PCBs and mercury. With over two hundred known toxic waste sites around the Great Lakes, compounds like these in the watershed caused the numbers of bald eagles, peregrine falcons and double-crested cormorants in this region to drop fast.

Fourteen years after Canada and the US signed the Great Lakes Water Quality Agreement in 1972, Hamilton City Council approved a Remedial Action Plan to try to reverse the damage done to air, earth and water. For instance, a fish barrier was built where the old Desjardins Canal cuts through the Iroquois Bar. The fishway, as it's called, is meant to keep the carp out of Cootes Paradise. It's a fascinating and strange thing to see this contraption in action. The fishway contains several wire cages about eight feet tall and six-by-six square. Each cage is an enormous lobster trap. The fish can swim in but not out. A winch as high as a small crane lifts the cages one by one out of the barrier and swings them over a sluice, where interns from the Royal Botanical Gardens sort out the arcs of flipping muscle at the bottom of the cage. A sign posted nearby lists the times each day when you can watch them lift the cages and sort out the fish. As the winch cranks each cage up into the air, the water pours out. The number of species at the bottom depends on the time of year. During the salmon and trout run in the spring, one of the interns told me, it's hectic at the fishway, with the interns counting as many as fifty gilled creatures. The times I've watched, though, there were only five or ten fish at the bottom of each cage. The intern opens a little door and the fish fall through it one by one and into the sluice. First, the intern notes the species of each one and, if it's a species they're keeping track of, weighs it. The sluice then divides in two directions: one pours into Cootes, the other into the canal, which runs into Hamilton Harbour. Trout, salmon, bass, perch and other native species are allowed entry into Cootes. Carp get stopped at the checkpoint and turned back to Lake Ontario.

The fishway is actually having the desired effect. When Wendy and I first put our canoe in Cootes six years ago, we'd jump out of our skins each time one of these roiling carp would slap the water with its large, flat tail. They're big fish – about two, two-and-a-half feet long. And they like to roll around in shallow water, stirring up the silt and vacuuming up every growing thing on the bottom. With them in the marsh, the number of water plants left in Cootes had dropped to only twenty-some species. We still see one or two carp when we canoe there now, but it's rare we get jolted by a tail flopping on the surface. With the carp on the wane, the RBG staff have been able to replant many marsh plants, including cattails, water lilies and wild rice.

They also stopped controlling water levels so fiercely. With a return to natural cycles wherein the mud flats get flooded and then bared to the sun, bog-type plants get a chance to germinate. RBG workers have also released native fingerlings into the water, so the numbers of native fish and plants are on the rise. Cootes Paradise is the spawning ground for twenty million fish fry, supplying half the fingerlings for all of Lake Ontario.

Cootes is the only spot within two hundred miles where Lake Ontario's shoreline has not been reconstructed to suit humans. With so many breakwaters, retaining walls, piers and landfills replacing what were once marshes, rocky coastlines or wetlands, there are few places at this end of the lake where fish can spawn. The result is that Lake Ontario has five percent of the fish it had a century ago. Nonetheless, the efforts to restore Cootes, along with tougher rules on what kinds of chemicals industries use, have begun to turn things around. Between 1981 and 1992, for example, mercury found in gull eggs in Hamilton Harbour fell sixty-nine percent, and between 1981 and 2004, DDE in those eggs dropped by ninety percent, while PCBs dropped by eighty-six percent. The twenty species of water plants in Cootes Paradise have multiplied into the thousands.

So the eagle has not yet landed – at least not at the top of our pine – but eagles are back in the neighbourhood. In fact, over the past two years, that pair of eagles hatched two sets of twin chicks. These ugly darlings have become local media celebrities, with baby, then toddler, then juvenile pictures appearing in the paper.

They have moved the nest a couple of times, but have settled, over the past couple of years, high up in a tall white pine.

Though I haven't seen one land yet on our broken pine, I have seen racoons up there. A big, solitary male shows up once every two weeks for a daylong snooze. We call him Broadbent, after the former leader of Canada's New Democratic Party, and in honour of the hump that shows up on every racoon's back – not to mention the sizeable breadth of this one's back end. Sometime after dusk, he clambers down the trunk to prowl the city's dumpsters, and we won't see him again for ten days or two weeks. We have also seen various mothers nursing their kits. If there's a litter, we'll see a grey and copper pile of fur on the sawed-off platform at the top. If it's just one kit, we'll see a couple of lumps up there. They'll wriggle and yawn every once in a while, or poke at their mom for a drink of milk. If it's summer and the sun gets too hot, they sometimes scramble out on a branch in search of shade, or climb down a rung or two where it's cooler.

Far from being a lookout for eagle eyes, then, our pine has turned into a flophouse for nocturnals. At least it's a place of peace.

ONERAHTASE'KO:WA PIERCES THE SKY. It reaches toward the sun. Very often, it's the tallest tree in the woods. It lifts people's thoughts to the way of peace under the Creator's sky.

Under the protection of the Tree of Peace, the Confederacy Council carries out its business. To this day, the eternal flame of the council fire is kept by the Onondagas, in the centre of council gatherings. The Kanien'kehá:ka and the Senecas, as elder brothers of the League, sit on the east, while the younger brothers, the smaller nations of Cayuga, Oneida and Tuscarora, sit together on the west. These orderly arrangements are intended to assure that people make decisions with a good mind, one that is clear and untroubled, that keeps the whole community, with all its differentiated parts, at the front of everyone's attention. A large white mat made from the feathery down of the globe thistle, symbolizing the purity and peace of the kayaneren'tsherakowa, is spread on the ground. A white wing is used to sweep away the dirt of discord that might foul the gathering place and confuse good thinking. A stick is used to chase away bugs, worms or other creeping disturbances that might approach the mat and interfere with long-range, clear thinking. All decisions must consider the implications for seven generations.

It's said, too, that an old leader is like a tree of peace. When a chief dies, it's common to say, "Another tree has fallen."

These practices show how concretely Hodinöhsö:ni' thinking is rooted in land, the actual physical place and what lives here in the community of its various members – human and more-than-human. It's sad and amazing to realize how much wisdom from this grounded, centuries-old knowledge has been overlooked. Take what early longhouse people knew about the fragrance of pine. Forest biologist Diana Beresford-Kroeger says that the distinct, resinous scent of pine is a natural antibiotic. This aerosol tang is the ester or alcohol form of pinosylvin, which stimulates breathing. It also functions as a mild narcotic that has an anaesthetic effect on your body and makes you feel relaxed. She says that a forest of pines sweeps the air, cleaning and "soporifying the atmosphere" wherever they grow.

In Japan, centuries of observing the uplift people get from walking in pinewood forests has generated the practice of *shinrin-yoku*, or forest bathing. In a 2007 study, Japanese researchers found that forest bathers' hostility and depression scores dropped significantly on days when they took a fifteen-minute walk among the pines. No wonder the Hodinöhsö:ni' call it the Tree of Peace. It literally relaxes you, helps you breathe deep, cleans the air. That's why, when there was terminal illness or death in the longhouse, the people burned white pine boughs. Though the Six Rafter people did not rationalize these practices with the language of science, they knew, through observation and experience, that the smoke's fungicidal properties could fight sickness and restore the spirit.

This is why it's called indigenous knowledge. It's the kind of wisdom that comes from knowing the place and its inhabitants, from knowing these things for a long time and observing how it all works over generations. The calm presence of an experienced elder is like pinosylvin in your lungs: when you lose an old one, it's as if you've lost a pine tree – there's anxiety and a shortness of breath. It's harder to think calmly and deliberately.

The Tree of Peace had this kind of calming effect on everything around it. The Hodinöhsö:ni' understood that it anchored the Dish with One Spoon. The nineteenth-century Seneca writer Arthur Parker says that after Peacemaker and the people had thrown their weapons into the watery hole and replanted onerahtase'ko:wa, he asked the people what they should do about hunting grounds. The assembled folks said, "We shall have one dish (or bowl) in which will be placed one beaver's tail and we shall all have coequal right to it, and there shall be no knife in it, for if there be a knife in it, there would be danger that it might cut someone and blood would thereby be shed." Thus, the dish has a spoon, but no knife.

For the Six Nations, the Tree of Peace defines the ideals of the Dish With One Spoon, where everybody can share the provisions of the earth without fear of an attack, or even of needing a visa. My friend and colleague at McMaster Rick Monture, who is Mohawk, says it represents something like the local supermarket – a co-operative one, where everybody can get what they need and feel welcome. The rules of participation are simple: use a Good Mind, which means, keep things orderly, don't threaten others, take only what you need and offer thanks for what you receive. The Dish is an ecological philosophy and a kind of international, interspecies diplomacy all in one, as humans are not the only members of the co-op, whose participants include everyone from Hano'gyeh the muskrat and A'nó:wara the turtle in the creation story to onerahtase'ko:wa the Tree of Peace. It's rooted in a specific, literal place, not just an abstract idea.

And we're in it.

When I first moved here nineteen years ago, I assumed the marsh was called Cootes Paradise after those water birds you see everywhere on marshes all over North America, the American coot. I was wrong. The coot from which the marsh got its name was not a bird but a Brit. His name was Lieutenant Thomas Coote, and in the eighteenth century he was an officer at the British fort on the Niagara River. According to *The Diary of Mrs. John Graves Simcoe: Wife of the First Lieutenant-Governor of the Province of Upper Canada, 1792–6,* Coote used to come to this valley to hunt water birds. The geese and ducks were so plentiful that he could sit in a chair with his gun somewhere near that fishway, where the Desjardins Canal would later be cut through the Iroquois Bar, and pick them out of the sky as they flew overhead. Niagara was overrun in those days with refugees from the American Revolutionary War, and Lieutenant Coote came here to indulge in a sport that also supplied desperate people with food.

Cootes Paradise was a crossroads. Anyone crossing the Niagara Peninsula from Lake Erie to the south or from the Niagara River to the east would have met up with travellers portaging from the Grand River watershed, which flows from the region of Lake Huron to the northwest. They'd have also met travellers skirting Lake Ontario from the northeast. Given the shelter of the escarpment cliffs, and waterfowl and wild rice below, Cootes was a natural place to rest and refill the hamper.

It would be important that it remain a peaceful place, where no one had to fear a knife hidden in the dish – which is why the French called the Attawandaron who lived here "Neutrals."

LIKE ANY OTHER LIVING thing, peace is fragile. You can kill it just as easily by neglect as by crushing it underfoot. You can't just make a law and expect that everyone will live happily ever after. Even if they share a dish with one spoon, people are people. We find ways to say we need a bit more from the dish – a bigger slice of the pie – than our neighbour. It's as if, when you name peace as your primary ideal, when you say out loud that it's your goal and destiny, unfolding history pulls the rug out from under your feet. Look at Jerusalem, the city of peace. Or all the peace we Canadians made in Afghanistan – and Somalia before that.

In much the same way, the descendants of those who invented the kayaneren'tsherakowa have had little peace over the last five hundred years. With the arrival of traders from Europe in this region in the seventeenth century, the Dish With One Spoon was thrown back into conflict, like it had been before the Peacemaker came. The Dutch, French and English newcomers had not been schooled in the kayaneren'tsherakowa, with its clan mothers choosing who could run for leadership, its democratic method for choosing leaders and making decisions, and the Dish's model of what we would now call a territorial commons. The sailors brought with them products, mechanisms and diseases – from rum to guns to smallpox – that devastated North America's population. Historians admit that they don't know exactly how many people lived in North America when Columbus arrived, but a common guess is around eighteen million. By the end of the nineteenth century, there were less than a million Indigenous people left in North America.

Rivalry over trading beaver pelts for things like muskets, iron kettles and axe heads sparked raiding and warfare between the Huronian and the Hodinöhsö:ni' confederacies. On the eastern border of their territory, the Mohawks battled the Mahicans to control trade with the Dutch and then the English down at the mouth of what's now known as the Hudson River. In the north and west, the Iroquoian Confederacy fought the Hurons over the French trade on the Great Lakes and St. Lawrence. They still called it the League of Peace, but that didn't stop them from overwhelming these trade rivals in the early eighteenth century, including the Neutrals in what used to be known as the Dish With One Spoon.

No sooner had the Hodinöhsö:ni' consolidated power in this region than the thirteen colonies rebelled against the British motherland. Despite their efforts to keep out of what to them looked like familial dispute between the fathers and sons, it became impossible to steer clear of the revolutionary conflict. Having proved their valour against the Hurons and their French allies, the Iroquois were seen, and saw themselves, as a fearsome force. Everybody wanted them on their side. Most members of the Hodinöhsö:ni' sided with their long-term British trading partners, while others supported the upstart colonists. The result is that members of the Six Nations took each other's lives as they found themselves on opposite sides of this fight between Britons.

Regardless of which side they supported, their crops were torched and their lands confiscated during the scorched-earth Clinton-Sullivan Campaign that George Washington sent to wipe out their homes in 1779. The surviving Hodinöhsö:ni' fled to the border country around Buffalo Creek (which dropped the creek from its name and, over the next century, grew into the city of Buffalo) and then broke up into various refugee parties that migrated to a variety of places. A large contingent, including people from all six of the Iroquoian nations, came with Thaientané:ken (Joseph Brant, a Kanien'kehá:ka officer in the British army) to the Grand River, where the British compensated them for their military contribution with almost a million acres, six miles on each side of the river from its source to its mouth at Lake Erie. Another group went to the Bay of Quinte on the north shore of Lake Ontario, not far from Peacemaker's birthplace. Some, mostly Oneida, ended up moving west of the thirteen colonies into what's now Wisconsin, while others filtered back quietly to their traditional lands around the Finger Lakes, particularly after the War of 1812, when hostilities between the United States and Britain began to cool.

Unable to avoid the newcomers' wars, the League of Peace broke into separated communities in a widespread diaspora.

WHEN HODINÖHSÖ:NI' ARE IN grief, when they've lost a leader or a loved one, they hold a ceremony they call "the Condolence." The Condolence comes from the story of Hyenwatha, which is how Rick Hill spells the chief's name. American poetry readers will have seen Longfellow spell it "Hiawatha," though the epic he made it into has little to do with the historical person from whom he got the name. Arthur Parker, who stayed closer to the original, spelled it "Ha-yĕnt-watha."

There are many places to start any story. So I'll begin with Hyenwatha's despair after his three daughters had been killed. He wandered off by himself, deep into the woods. His heart sank to ground. He saw death everywhere, heard death everywhere, tasted death everywhere. Iroquoian stories, like most Indigenous oral narratives, are strikingly specific about where things happened. It's usually more important to tell *where* an event took place than to specify when. According to Baptist Thomas's version of the story, Hyenwatha's solitary wandering brought him eventually to the area around what's now known as Tully Lake in New York State. There, watching the lake reeds bend in the breeze, he saw so many small tubular shells strewn along the shores of the water that he gathered a deerskin full of them. He strung these shells together and hung three strings of them on a pole placed across two uprights. As he did this, he felt his scrambled thoughts untangling, being laid out in order, one by one.

"This is good," he thought. "But I wish someone could come and help me with the grief I'm carrying. I wish someone would take strings of shells like these from my hand and speak aloud my words of sorrow. The beads would order my thoughts one by one and untangle the confusion."

This incident is said to have sparked the Hodinöhsö:ni' use of wampum – a system of carefully weaving beads into patterned strings and belts that organize and record important words and messages. It's also the origin of the Condolence ceremony. For it was there, at the border of the dark wood, just as Hyenwatha was unfolding these thoughts, that Peacemaker came to him. Just as the grieving man had hoped, Peacemaker is said to have taken the strings of wampum from his makeshift rack and spoken the comforting, gentle words that were ordered and shaped by the strings of beads. One thought at a time. No confusion. No on-rush of too many thoughts at once. No welter of emotions. Just one by one, the words Hyenwatha needed to hear.

Following the outline of this story, the Hodinöhsö:ni' still condole those who have suffered the loss of someone important in their community by having those from other communities come to the edge of the village clearing where those who mourn live. At the edge of the woods, the place where dark meets bright, where the welter of branches and bush gives way to open air and sunlight, the two groups meet in ceremony. Elder Tom Porter (whose Mohawk name is Sakoweniónkwas) explains that it's at the edge of the woods that the Roti'nikonhrakáhte, the community members whose minds are strong and upright, come to lift up the Roti'nikonhrakwenhtará:'on, whose minds have fallen flat upon the ground. The edge marks the place where those who are standing come to wipe the tears from the eyes so filled with death they can't see anything else. They come through the woods from other horizons to remind those who grieve that the sun still rises and the seasons still complete their cycles. And as they offer these reminders, they use three strings of wampum to clear the vision of those blinded by grief, to free the passages of the ears that can't hear, to unblock the lump in throats that cannot speak.

It's significant then, that our broken pine, right here in our yard, stands at the woods' edge. Another tree has fallen. At least, a large part of it has. We live in a time of loss, a time of grief, a time of brokenness, when the elders are missing and the order of things is in disarray.

The people grieving the loss of their homes in the Finger Lakes area desperately needed Condolence after they arrived from Buffalo Creek in 1784. In recognition of their military service during the war, Governor Haldimand granted them a piece of the Dish with One Spoon along the banks of the river here in lands the British had recently bought from the Anishinaabe Michi Saagiig (known in English as the Mississaugas). It must have been comforting to hear there was a new home to move to.

But there was little time to wipe away tears, because the claim the Hodinöhsö:ni' had to their new home was a back and forth thing. That's the trouble with a grant – it undermines your independence. You're supposed to be grateful to whoever granted it to you, and even if it was given in recognition of your sacrifice, of how you lost family and home by siding with your British allies

– even though everyone knows without saying so that your allies may not have survived at all in North America without you – it's still not easy to set your own terms for how big the grant should be and how exclusive your rights to it are.

The million acres on both sides of the Grand River granted by Haldimand was cut by one third in 1792 by Lieutenant Governor John Graves Simcoe. It was cut even more by disputed land leases and sales conducted by Brant with less-than-stellar land dealers like Richard Beasley, and cut again when suspiciously few Confederacy Council chiefs signed away another big section in 1841. Some historians, like Charles Johnson, suspect those chiefs were coerced. Whatever your view of these losses, it's a fact that by 1850, seventy years after they arrived, the Hodinöhsö:ni' had only forty-seven thousand acres left, less than five percent of the original Haldimand Tract. Nobody has been found guilty of fraud or land theft. Every reduction was found by British and then Canadian officials to be legal, consistently fair and square.

And the legal whittling continues.

Because there are so many irregularities over sales, leases and expropriations of land in the two hundred years since the Hodinöhsö:ni' refugees arrived on the Grand River, the Band Council established a Six Nations Land Claims Research Office in the 1970s. After twenty years of wrangling with the government, this office issued a report on *Outstanding Financial and Land Issues* in 1997. According to this report, between 1974 and 1994, the Six Nations Land Claims Research Office had filed concerns with the Crown over twenty-seven pieces of land. These concerns indicated that disputed leases had been treated as outright sales, sales slips had been signed by people who were long-since dead and Indian agents had somehow ended up with title to reserve land. Of these twenty-seven, one was resolved in 1980 and four others were acknowledged by Canada's Justice Department as needing resolution. The remaining files were simply closed by Indian and Northern Affairs Canada in 1995 without having been looked into.

Among the disregarded files was one that has since become notorious. Registered with the government on June 18, 1987, it fingered a piece of land that had been requisitioned by the British government in order to build the Hamilton-Port Dover Plank Road. Basically, the Six Nations said these 7,680 acres had been *leased* to the province in the nineteenth century for the road running through the reserve from Lake Ontario to Lake Erie, while the provincial government said that the lands had been *sold*. Instead of looking into and clarifying the original arrangements, the province went ahead and resold it. A sizeable piece went in 1992 to a company called Henco Industries. The developer planned to build a two-hundred-home housing development called Douglas Creek Estates between the town of Caledonia and the Six Nations Reserve.

Troubled by seeing bulldozers and concrete mixers at work on disputed land, several young Hodinöhsö:ni' women decided to reassert Six Nations' concerns about the land on which Douglas Creek Estates would be built. Handing out leaflets to passing cars on Highway 6, the old plank road, had little effect. So on February 26, 2006, they made a firepit on the land and set some lawn chairs around it. They sat in blankets and sleeping bags around the clock, while smoke rose up in the winter air. Their purpose was to stop the bulldozers and trucks from carrying on with their work. The reclaimers said the land had never been surrendered or sold, and demanded that building stop until a settlement could be reached between the Six Nations and the federal and provincial governments.

In a country whose economy is determined by indexes such as building starts and the housing market, construction can never cease. Slowing down "development" isn't an option. It's not even a conversation. It's as if the idea of interrupting the expansion of urban construction is against our economic religion.

It wasn't hard, then, for Henco Industries to secure a court injunction requiring the reclaimers to leave the property. And on April 20, 2006, after they refused to leave, the Ontario Provincial Police sent in two hundred officers armed with M16s, tear gas, pepper spray and Tasers. Sixteen people were arrested in the ensuing dust-up. Despite the heavy artillery, however, Hodinöhsö:ni' from the reserve turned up in such large numbers that the police eventually backed off and the reclaimers kept control of the site. Patrols from Six Nations have stayed there ever since.

I remember those days clearly, because as I walked into my office at the university around midday on April 20, ascending from the Ancaster Creek valley, crossing the overpass that spans Cootes Drive and turning the corner of the Mary Keyes building, I was startled to see twenty or thirty police cars parked in the sheltered driveway behind the building and out of sight from the main roadway. Not having heard yet about the police raid early that morning, I assumed that perhaps the OPP had rented out a campus residence for a conference or convention, now that students had decamped for the summer. It wasn't until later in the day that I heard from Six Nations colleagues on campus that

McMaster was serving as the barracks for the police who had raided the site.

Things are never as straightforward as they look. Although Six Nations people have good reasons to be angry about the legal trickery by which they lost land that should be theirs, there are many layers to the standoff – not least of which is that at the height of tensions in 2006, the Mohawk Warriors showed up. Now, there are warriors and there are warriors. When the Confederacy was established, there was a role for young men whose duty was to defend their elders, women and children from danger. You might think of them as their society's police. And there are fire circles to this day that train young men to be protectors of the community. After two hundred years of having sections of their homeland expropriated and removed by Canada's legal system, you can understand why the longhouse people would want their own police, their own legal system, their own protection.

But what has also happened in the meantime is that the cigarette trade between tax-free reserves in the USA and tax-free reserves in Canada has encouraged the emergence of a different kind of warrior. These are warriors who protect, not so much elders and women, but the ambiguously legal cigarette trade and other clearly illegal cross-border smuggling operations. These warriors can be heavily armed, and they don't always have licences for each and every gun they carry. The presence of these black market warriors alongside the fire-circle warriors provokes the government to send in even more heavily armed police and special detective squads. Witnesses at the 2006 standoff discovered the American FBI poking around in what was supposed to be a Canadian land dispute.

Violence has broken out many times in the years since, between the Hodinöhsö:ni' patrolling the site and flag-waving Canadians who have staged protests against the reclaimers. At times it's gotten downright ugly. Some of the Canadian protesters have been members of the neo-Nazi skinhead crowd. There have been fist fights, stones thrown and curses exchanged. The two sides have been playing a dead earnest game of Capture the Flag – except instead of capturing the other team's flag, Canadian zealots have tried to plant the Maple Leaf at the Hodinöhsö:ni' camp on the Douglas Creek Estates.

To avoid further violence that might see Caledonia turned into another Ipperwash Crisis, where the police underwent a long investigation after they shot and killed the native protestor Dudley George, the OPP have changed tactics. After their first raid came to grief, they backed off and have tried to maintain a buffer zone between white protestors and the Six Nations reclaimers at the site. Given the presence of white neo-Nazis, the warriors and who knows how many kinds of police, it's sheer luck that nobody has been killed. The OPP's new tactics have been seen by some of the Maple Leaf planters as playing favourites with the Hodinöhsö:ni' reclaimers who, according to the court injunction, were supposed to leave the site. In the meantime, the Ontario government bought the land from Henco Industries and put it in trust until a settlement can be reached between the Confederacy Chiefs Council of the Six Nations and the two levels of government. These many years later, negotiations are pretty much dead in the water.

WE LIVE, THEN, IN the shelter of a splintered tree of peace at the woods' edge.

Our pine is a strange and twisted thing. But it's absolutely thriving. Its branches grow long and heavy. They bristle with huge cones. Its clutches of five long needles haven't stopped making chlorophyll. They're still turning carbon into oxygen. This battered tree is literally putting life in our lungs.

It's pretty fascinating to see what's happening in these early years of the twenty-first century, because Hamilton is undergoing a significant transition. Not all that long ago, in a November 28, 2008, *Hamilton Spectator* article, Rachel De Lazzer linked our city's high poverty rates to air pollution. At that time, sixteen percent of Hamiltonians lived in poverty – that was one out of every six. Almost one in four children went to school hungry each day. She reported that in 2005, Hamilton produced 2,240,453 kilos of airborne pollutants like lead and mercury. If we add killers like sulphur dioxide to other toxins that make smog and acid rain, Hamilton pumped 58,788,549 kilos of pollutants into the air that same year. The article claimed the obvious: the city's high poverty rates were linked to the polluted water and air, which kept housing costs down. People didn't want to live in a fouled environment, so they didn't want to live in our city. Those who remained did so only because they could afford the rent.

I remember thinking at the time that I was glad our city was affordable, that people who needed a relatively inexpensive place to live were given a second or a third chance – but not at the expense of fouled air. Hamilton's situation, however, has been changing quickly since 2008. It's now more than twenty years since the steel industry slowed down in this city, and while former Stelco workers are still fighting to get the new owner to honour their pensions, Hamilton's economy has shifted to other sectors, especially high tech and healthcare companies.

With the steel industry running at a fraction of its former capacity, air quality in the city has improved significantly. I remember fifty days in a row of official smog warnings in the summer of 2005. I can't remember a single smog warning in the past three or four summers. Hamilton's real estate is cheap by Toronto standards, which has generated an out-migration of Torontonians seeking properties in Hamilton, with the result that housing prices are going up quickly in our city. According to a May 20, 2016, *Spectator* article by Steve Arnold, the average house price in our city was $270,000 in January 2012, whereas by May 2016 it had risen to $430,000, an increase of sixty-two percent. These increases in property values put pressure on low-income housing, where available rental units have dropped to 3.2 percent this year and are expected to drop to 2.9 percent in 2017. This, in a city where Tom Cooper of the Hamilton Roundtable for Poverty Reduction notes that ten percent of the population still lives on social assistance. So poor people still live in Hamilton, but not because housing is cheap here.

There's nothing we can do now about the broken pine. There's no chance it can be fixed and grow again to its original height or shape. No eagle watches from its satellite dish of a top. The League of Peace is scattered, its dispersed members embroiled in various disputes both internal and external. The water that feeds its roots is tainted by pollutants that don't just vanish after the brown clouds thin from our increasingly blue sky.

This tree did not fall, but it's certainly been wounded. It marks the place at the edge of the woods, the place to bring your tears, the place for condolence.

For all this, the wounded pine hums with life. It makes oxygen and pinosylvin from the less-than-perfect air. Its aerosols fight cancer of every kind. It throws shade over its white roots, which fan out in all directions. They pull dirty water up to the magic of sunlight. If you want to see how it's done, just follow them. Despite the huge scar across its trunk, despite the splintering and the saw, despite a whole lot of trauma, the Tree of Peace and the Dish with One Spoon can still be tracked and found. They're right here in this ground, still flickering in the eyes of people hungry for peace, power and righteousness. Every day, this stunted pine in the midst of this city puts the air I need in my lungs. Its branches house squirrels, woodpeckers, chickadees, wrens, the occasional owl. It gives raccoons a couch to crash on.

It not only survives, it grows.

Every day, this broken pine makes and remakes a place to live in, a place to belong. It digs deeper into the ground, twists its weird branches higher into the light, adds another ring to its girth. It makes the most of its reality. Every day, it shows us how to live here, the only way anyone can anywhere – by breathing every day, shaping ourselves to the place where we are planted, each day making life.

Deer in Their
Own Coats

The deer were going directly into a human community, upon their own volition. Why?

It is a question I cannot answer, but it is a manner of accommodation. It reminded me of my Indian people of the past. They too went into the white-man's community, putting on his coat and tie, and attempting to accommodate to this strange society. The result was mixed. Some survived, most didn't.

Did the deer survive? Probably. I don't know. [They] were wearing their own coats.

– Oren Lyons, "Power of the Good Mind"

THIS SIGHTING OF URBAN deer took place in Syracuse, New York, about three hundred kilometres east of where I live in Hamilton. The renowned Onondaga chief and university professor Oren Lyons was driving home late one night after a long day at the office where he worked at SUNY Buffalo as Chair of American Studies. Just after he'd passed a large cemetery, he braked to watch two does and a yearling tiptoe across the road and vanish into the hedges and lawns of a suburb. Instead of sticking to the safety of the woods, the deer crossed the road right in front of his car and walked, unpressured and unbidden, into the city. Reflecting on the Hodinöhsö:ni' respect for the equal value of all lives, Lyons writes: "We must see with the clarity of those animals that live among us ... and we must reciprocate their interaction."

I too have been watching a family of urban deer in the woods below our street and above the university parking lots. I fiddle with the focus on my binoculars, so I can see the lights in this curious fawn's eyes, the shine on her moist nose, the steam coming out of her nostrils. She's close – about twenty-five metres away. She stares hard at me. Her ears stare, too.

Then she nods her head, very in your face: down, then up.

Again: Down. Then up.

In between nods, she stamps one of her dainty-looking hooves into the inch of snow. Huff! Deer commonly look shy, high-strung and nervous, so the aggression in her actions makes me jump. She glares hard at me throughout this sequence. As if we're in a staring contest.

Down. Then up.

After several nods and stamps, she blasts air loudly through her nostrils. I'm guessing it means "Hey, you, Git!" Or, to her family behind her, "He's still here!"

The sound is so sharp and unexpected I jump again.

She bows again.

What does all this mean? Maybe I should reciprocate.

So I bow. Down. Then up. Very big movements, very dramatic – not just a little tilt of the head. I bow from the waist to match the long arc of her motion, like they do in Shakespeare. I try to match the formality and size of her movements, but without the aggression.

I don't stamp, but I do a little blow. Fuff! I'm serious about this. I mean no disrespect.

But she seems to think that either I'm mocking her or she's made her point, because she gives another disdainful huff with her hoof then turns and vaults over the fallen tree behind her.

The beauty of her motion gives the impression that deer take something like comportment classes in their youth. A perfect half-circle in the air. Hooves lifted, formal and curled, at the ankle. The half-circle of the vault exactly the same radius from its centre, as if someone had drawn it with a compass. The landing, soft and dignified, with just the right amount of give so that nothing jars or jiggles. The whole arcing movement has the grace of slow motion. As soon as it's over, I want to rewind and watch it again.

This young one's sudden vault startles the rest of the clan, and they trot after her across the swampy ground and into the trees on the other side.

We've had some kind of interaction, but I don't know what it meant. I hope my bowing and snorting didn't mean something bad about her mother.

I had heard or read somewhere that hoof stamping is an alarm signal, but I assumed it was an auditory thing, perhaps reinforced by vibrations in the ground that other deer can feel. I didn't know until reading up on deer communication that it also works by smell. It turns out white-tailed deer have what they call interdigital glands, located between the two halves of each hoof. A sharp jab into the earth releases some yellow waxy stuff with a strong odour. What I thought were dainty jabs were actually stink bombs.

I don't know how effective hoof jabbing would be in winter. Would the soft snow underfoot cushion the impact and release of the smelly wax? Would the smell be lost in the cold? I didn't smell anything, and even when I ran over to where she'd been, I saw no sign of wax. Maybe it was buried in the snow somewhere. To me, the hoof stomping looked cute, like a child not getting her way.

Smell is central in deer communication. Not only do white-tails have scent glands between the toes of their hooves, they also have them on the outside of what looks like their ankle but is technically called the metatarsal joint. They've got another set on the insides of their knees, technically the tarsal or, in horse language, the hock.

When I first started watching the deer, I couldn't help but no-tice they all have round, black, leathery-looking patches on the insides of their hocks. If you look at a deer head-on, you'll see they have a slightly knock-kneed stance, especially in the long, slim, back legs. So I had wondered if the black leather patches were spots – calluses, you might say – where the fur gets worn away by constant rubbing when they walk.

Not at all. These tarsal, metatarsal and interdigital glands are all parts of their communications system. All they have to do is walk and their hoof glands leave wax signs of their passing on the ground. And whenever they drag an ankle through the leaves of a shrub, or when their knees rub each other, they're expressing themselves. They're communicating all the time – a whole sys-tem of sentience and feeling that exceeds our notice.

I've seen it at other times of the year too, but especially dur-ing breeding season, bucks will create "rubs" or "scrapes." They'll arch their backs awkwardly and pee so that it runs over the black leather patches of their tarsal glands and down into muddy patches that they have scraped up with their hooves. With all that pee and musk, their ballsiness is pretty hard for other bucks, and interested does, to misread. The males will also scrape bark and twigs from small trees with their antlers, leaving behind scent from their heads on the trunks while polishing their boney spars. Then they'll mix these tree bits into their urine-and-musk-scented soup.

I don't have a great sense of smell. There have been times when I've been down in the deer grounds and the place reeked of what I think was deer rub. But there is also leakage from household and street drains that seeps down below our neighbourhood, and I'd be hard-pressed to tell deer communication from the odour of fetid water, and then to differentiate between both of these and the compost of rotting vegetation that's part of any swampy area.

AND WHAT WOULD OREN LYONS think about the six-foot-high chain-link fence we built around our backyard to keep out these interactive, always-communicating deer?

Before we installed the fence, we really couldn't keep plants growing in the garden. A sharp, horizontal line on our cedar hedge about six feet from the ground used to mark how high deer can reach. Above this line, a luxurious-looking tuft of sappy, thick green poked stiffly into the air. Below it, like one of those posters in a doctor's waiting room showing the human nervous system, you could see where deer teeth had exposed the grey-brown tangle of ribs, gnarled and brittle. I couldn't imagine cedar as tasty, so I tried some. The resin was sharp as gasoline. My eyes ran, nose and mouth instantly flooding. But maybe winter hunger, and their knowledge of vitamins, makes cedar necessary when the snow is deep.

Maybe it was generations of watching deer that taught the Hodinöhsö:ni' to cure the scurvy killing Jacques Cartier's sailors in the 1530s with cedar tea.

The deer were on their way to killing the euonymus hedge on the east side of our yard. It was as if they were tossing their own winter salad: a mouthful of fumy cedar, then a mild green euonymus leaf or two, followed by another hit of cedar. Every spring, tulips would unwrap swelling green buds and, just as the first signs of colour streaked their casings, I'd come out in the morning to find stem after stem beheaded, tulip sap leaking from the cut.

We tried to share. To be good neighbours and live in harmony. We checked the web to find out how to keep the deer from eating our favourite plants. One idea was to pare off shavings of strong-smelling Irish Spring soap and spread them around our plants. When that didn't work, we tried mothballs, clustered at the roots like partridge eggs. Their astringency made our eyes water in the garden. We tried shaking powdered chili pepper onto the hosta leaves. The pepper made an ugly oxblood stain down the middle of each green and white leaf. And the deer seemed to like the pepper.

One website suggested we put out pails of coyote pee, which they could supply through the mail. I tried to imagine the look on the delivery guy's face when he asked me to sign for it.

After reading through our plant books and visiting the garden centre, we came home with narcissus bulbs and spiky, inedible-looking holly bushes to replace the tulips and hostas. Animals know narcissus are poison, so the next spring the daffodils and hyacinths did not get cropped off. But the holly was soon as chewed up as the hostas and the coralbells.

Deer are like goats – they'll eat anything. Not only will they eat flowers, fruit or acorns, white-tailed deer have been known to feed on nesting songbirds and field mice. Good luck finding garden plants they don't like.

Now we have the fence, and we can grow things again. There was a readjustment period, when our white-tailed neighbours grudgingly gave up their quest for our cedar hedge. Early the first winter after we installed the fence, we were surprised to find a doe grazing contentedly on the euonymus hedge one morning. In a way, I was glad to see her. I had wanted to see if deer could get into the yard and, if they could, whether they could get out again on their own. I didn't want the new fence to create a trap. So I put on my boots and ran out into the yard hollering. She took off down the slope and did that gorgeous half-moon vault right over the fence at the bottom, her perfect hooves just clipping the top rail.

But how did she get in? The inch of snow let me follow her tracks back to the eight-inch gap between our fence post and the corner of our neighbour's carport. You'd never dream that a four-foot-tall, one-hundred-twenty-pound adult animal could squeeze through the tiny gap.

These euonymus leaves must be delicious. I had tasted the cedar, so I thought I might as well taste one of these. At first bite, it had the texture and flavour of a plastic bag. After a few seconds, it released a slight, short-lasting bitterness. Not entirely unpleasant, but not as distinctive as arugula or dandelion, not as crunchy as iceberg or romaine. Maybe it's more appealing when you live outside all winter and can't run to a store full of hothouse greens.

That encounter with the doe in the yard is a few years ago now, and we haven't had one since. Today, you can see a clear path following our fence, where they cross the valley below our row of houses, looking for water from the springs down there and easier pickings from our fenceless neighbours' yards. Maybe our chain-link makes us good neighbours.

I HAVEN'T BEEN THE only one keeping an eye on the deer in this city.

In November 2009, the Hamilton Conservation Authority closed the Iroquoia Heights Conservation Area, up on the lip of the escarpment two kilometres from here, after a fellow taking photos came across the intestines of a deer that had been butchered right there, in the city park. According to the paper, he also found a carbon arrow outfitted with razor-sharp blades.

A day or two later, park workers saw a Six Nations man carrying a crossbow in the same park. Upon inquiry, he said he was conducting "an environmental scan."

So began a string of articles in the *Hamilton Spectator* on the overpopulation of deer in the city, the treaty rights of Hodinöhsö:ni' people to hunt all over this region and the idea of "deer management." Another version of the idea of water management.

Around the time of the disembowelled deer at Iroquoia Heights, members of the Hodinöhsö:ni' Wildlife and Habitat Authority contacted the Hamilton Conservation Authority to inform them that there were too many deer for the 120-hectare park.

The Ministry of Natural Resources did an aerial survey of Iroquoia Heights and agreed with the Hodinöhsö:ni' Wildlife and

Habitat Authority. They counted 102 deer in an area that should feed a dozen or less. They also found similar overpopulations of whitetails throughout Hamilton's park system. Iroquoia Heights is under particular pressure because it's boxed in by roads and neighbourhoods. The six lanes of Highway 403 slice up the side of the escarpment in a half-circle that hems in the north and west sides of the park. At the top, hundreds of thousands of roaring cars and trucks braid into that cloverleaf where the 403 connects to the four lanes of the Lincoln Alexander Parkway, also known as the Linc, which cuts off access on the south side. The only way deer can get in or out of the park is through the suburb at the end of Mohawk Road.

Note all the Hodinöhsö:ni' names: Niagara Escarpment, Iroquoia Heights, Mohawk Road. Like the Brant Johnson family's original ownership of the land we live on, these names remind us how this whole area is saturated with Six Nations presence, whether we're conscious of it or not. Often, it's camouflaged, power-dressed in the suit and tie of politics and bureaucracy: a Hodinöhsö:ni' Wildlife and Habitat Authority to match the Hamilton Conservation Authority. And sometimes it emerges from the government-to-government negotiations of the Indian Affairs regime, when negotiators in Ottawa insist on wearing their own coats.

Without predators, or ready entry or exit, the whitetails of Iroquoia Heights have reproduced phenomenally. The park is like a test tube, a reproduction laboratory.

With the Ministry's confirmation that there were too many deer in the parks, the Hamilton Conservation Authority tried to corral the situation by holding closed-door talks with Six Nations hunters about organizing a cull. Suddenly one day, hiking trails in a section of the Dundas Valley, west of Iroquoia Heights, sprouted signs announcing a deer hunt was underway and people should proceed with caution.

Proceed? With caution?

Letters to the newspaper had a field day. How would the park managers guard against accidents? Would the Iroquoian hunters avoid dogs or children? One woman said she was going to buy a construction worker's orange safety vest for her Great Dane – it was too dangerous for her dog to wear his own, unmarked coat.

For a while, the debate focused on the Treaty of Albany of 1701, commonly called the Nanfan Treaty after John Nanfan, British governor of New York when the treaty was signed. In this agreement, the Hodinöhsö:ni' Confederacy recalled their victories over the Hurons between the 1640s and 1660s in what is now Ontario north of the Great Lakes. They then signed over to the British exclusive trading rights throughout a huge tract of land north of the Ohio River, from what's now upstate New York all the way to Chicago. This swath of land covered much of southern Ontario. In exchange, they demanded perpetual hunting and fishing rights throughout the whole region. Never mind that this was not exactly where the Hurons had lived, so it wasn't really Confederacy territory to sign away. Never mind that by this time the Anishinaabek had pushed them out of much of the land now known as Ontario. Some have suggested that the Hodinöhsö:ni' were playing two sides of the treaty game, signing the Great Peace of Montréal to make peace with the French and their Algonquian allies during the same summer that they signed the Nanfan Treaty with the British.

Whatever the politics of the day, Ontario's attorney general
and the Minister of Aboriginal Affairs ruled, in response to the
Hamilton Conservation Authority's inquiry in June 2011, that
the Nanfan Treaty still applies in the twenty-first century. By
this time, the Conservation Authority had quickly put together
what they called the Deer Management Advisory Committee.
A member of this group told the *Spectator* that "the hunting
rights are not ... HCA's to give or take away. They are rights the
Hodinöhsö:ni' already possess. No one is allowed to deny them
these rights."

Canadians tend to know, in a fuzzy way, that treaties were
signed somewhere back in history and that they have something
to do with why First Nations live on reserves and we have the rest
of the land, but most people seem to think the treaties somehow
went out of fashion and lost their legal clout. So it was more than
a shock for many Hamiltonians to learn that a treaty signed in
1701 is still binding and that it gives the descendants of its longhouse signatories the right to hunt in our city.

Treaty or not, people were affronted at the idea of hunting
going on in city parks. In May 2010, the racial underbelly of that
outrage rose to the surface. The *Spectator* reported that a Conservation Authority ecologist had been doing a deer survey in
Iroquoia Heights when she spotted a deer bone. Her discovery
made her check the area more closely, and what she found was
an animal pit trap, complete with upright sticks and a plywood
cover, hidden by a camouflage net and a dusting of leaves. Residents in the neighbourhood said they'd seen another one in the
park. These dangerous traps were immediately linked to "sus-
pected native hunting." The ecologist said, "You could probably

break something [if you fell in].... You could get bruised, broken, or you could get impaled by a stick." The same article quoted the director of the Animal Alliance of Canada saying that people who live near the park sent her photos of a camouflaged pit and a shotgun shell. These two pieces of evidence were about six metres apart in the conservation area.

The implication was that Native hunters have no concern for Hamiltonians' safety. The recognition of Indigenous treaties makes everyday citizens susceptible to physical harm as First Nations use outdated treaties to sabotage our civil order.

But it turns out this was not the whole story. The very next day, the *Spectator* printed a photo of a ten-year-old boy from the neighbourhood beside Iroquoia Heights. The boy reported that he and a couple of friends had built a fort in the conservation area by fitting poles into a sinkhole and covering it with a plywood roof. He'd saved up his allowance until he had the fifty dollars he needed to buy a camouflage net to keep the fort hidden. He and his friends squirreled away cool stuff in their dugout, like binoculars and a bullet casing.

"We'd rather be outside than playing Xbox," he said.

I'VE STARTED TO MAKE regular visits to what I've come to call the deer yard in the valley below our place. Mostly, I go down to the marshy spot that used to be Binkley's Pond. It's part of the living lab the McMarsh group want to restore to its natural state.

I've never been a hunter; I am not a wildlife biologist, either by training or instinct, and, until recently, I've never tried to get to know whitetails. But it seems they've insisted that I pay attention to them, not just by chewing my tulips and forcing me to build a fence, but also by asserting themselves in Hamilton's streets and city parks. With them creating an uproar in our city's political life, it's become harder and harder to ignore them.

Urban people consider it strange that deer are living in such numbers in our neighbourhoods. But then, why is it such a surprise? What made us assume that a city would be a place where the only neighbours would be other people? These hooved neighbours are making us scratch our heads. They're insisting upon our notice. But what are they saying? And, to echo Oren Lyons, how do we reciprocate their interaction?

So, over the past winter, I started visiting the deer yard as often as I could, trying to see if I could learn something about how they live in my neighbourhood, seeing how I might reciprocate. Whatever that means. When you're an utter novice, you start where you can.

The first time I tried to sneak unnoticed down to the deer yard, I was disappointed to see they'd known I was coming long before I saw them. As I say, deer have a keen nose. I therefore checked the breeze and saw it was coming from the southwest, and I crept up to the yard from the east. I felt pretty smart about that – and about thinking to wear beige and brown clothing to match the winter woods. But I learned later that deer are dichromatic, meaning that they see a two-colour spectrum and not the three-colour spectrum that humans see. This must be why hunters don't mind wearing Day-Glo orange hats or lime-green safety vests. What deer do see, and better than humans, are patterns and changes in texture. Two-colour vision works better in shady woods than three-colour because the forest canopy dulls colour, draining the light from reds, bright greens and other lively colours. Deer pay attention to changes in pattern, where our tri-colour vision causes us to notice varieties of colour.

Deer also have excellent ears. White centred and outlined in black fur, they swivel like small radar dishes and can pivot independently from each other. White-tailed deer can hear about five or six times better than humans can. I tried not to snap twigs as I tread on the frozen, snowless ground, but I needn't have bothered – they could hear everything about my approach, from my jacket sleeves rustling against the sides of my body to my breathing. I've since figured out that new soft snow, plus a whistling wind or something else, like traffic noise, help to mask my lumbering through the woods. However, I hadn't thought about these things then.

So when I poked my head over the ridge above the low, spongy ground on my first visit to the deer yard, the two bucks, two does and three younger ones already had their heads up and were staring at me. The two bucks had their antlers. I'd read enough to know that their presence with the does meant that they were still in rutting season. Once they get to be one-and-a-half or two years old, males separate off from the does and fawns except for mating season. They may hang out with each other in bachelor groups in the spring and early summer, but otherwise bucks are pretty much loners.

Deer are distinguished from antelope by having antlers made of bone, which they shed every winter and regrow through the spring and summer. By contrast, antelope have fibre horns that they never shed. The new antlers prepare whitetail bucks for sparring over females in the fall rut. One of the two bucks in the deer yard was clearly older, with a big barrel chest, a large apron of white fur under his chin and a six-point rack of antlers about two feet across and eighteen inches high. The smaller one also had six-points, but his antlers were about eighteen inches across and about a foot tall. His chest and thighs were slimmer, less bullish. From what I've read, bucks are supposed to drop their antlers after the fall rut, but these two still had theirs in January, and as I watched their yard over the next months, I saw the younger one still had his antlers in early March. So they must not follow the guidebooks about when to shed their antlers.

Deer hold an honoured place in Hodinöhsö:ni' creation stories. Following the story about Atsi'tsiaká:ion falling from the Sky World and landing on A'nó:wara's hard shell comes the story of how Sky Woman's daughter died giving birth to twins. The first twin had been born normally, but the second was too impatient to wait his turn, so he burst out of his mother's armpit, killing her in the process. Ever since, the two sons have been in conflict. The peaceable twin, Shonkwaya'tíson, created humans and all the upright, beautiful creatures by breathing into their carthen bodies, while the restless twin, Shawískara (sometimes spelled Tawískaron), trying to outdo his brother's creations, made incomplete, crawling and monstrous beings. Their rivalry escalated from gambling games to stickball competitions and, eventually, into outright fighting. All the earth's creatures watched the battle rage day after day. The generous-hearted brother knew that there were only two things that his jealous brother feared: flint stone and deer antlers. Finally, after many days of struggle,

Ohskennón:ton, the stag, lowered his head to the ground and gave his antlers to the first brother, who used them to push his unhappy brother over the edge and into the underworld.

Deer are therefore revered in Hodinöhsö:ni' tradition for being generous supporters and protectors of the good mind and the creative spark of life. They gave their antlers to the creator of good things to help him overcome selfishness and resolve conflict, and they continue to give their coats and bodies to keep humans clothed and fed. To this day, Hodinöhsö:ni' leaders wear deer antlers in their headdresses to remind everybody how peaceable relations depend on the good mind.

This part of the story encouraged me to keep an eye out for antlers whenever I've gone to visit the deer yard. Bucks drop them every year, so it shouldn't be too hard to find some. It would signify an interaction. I've looked and looked. So far, no luck. The floor of the yard is littered with deadfalls from the maples and walnuts whose grey-white branches are exactly the colour of bone, so it's a little like looking for a needle in a haystack.

OVER THE NEXT TWO years, the Deer Management Advisory Committee consulted with the Six Nations Confederacy, the Animal Alliance of Canada, the Ministry of Natural Resources and Forestry, the provincial Minister of Aboriginal Affairs, city aldermen and folks who live in the neighbourhood of Iroquoia Heights. Pretty much everyone agreed there were too many deer in the city, but they had very different views about what to do about it. Residents in the neighbourhood said the deer were crowding into their yards, eating plants, pooping in their gardens and, according to one person, "chasing terrified residents from their own decks." I can imagine how a full-grown buck with a large rack of antlers might scare some people, but most deer are not exactly fearsome.

Some warned that an overpopulation of deer creates environmental imbalance. They pointed to cedar trees stripped of their bark and the way numbers of white trilliums had dropped off in the conservation lands around Hamilton. In 2006 alone, the Ministry of Natural Resources and Forestry counted two hundred deer-related car crashes in the Hamilton area, and they guessed that seventy-five percent of these kinds of crashes never get reported. Others who attended the Deer Management Advisory Committee meetings said they'd seen deer blinds and little pieces of fluorescent tape to gauge shooting distance tied to bushes in the valley. They'd also found headless dear carcasses – all signs that poachers were active in the city.

But what to do? Representatives of the Ontario Federation of Anglers and Hunters suggested a radical culling. As you can imagine, the Animal Alliance of Canada strongly objected. A kill is short sighted, they argued, because populations wiped out quickly rebound quickly. Their solution, though, sounded weak: start a public education campaign to teach people not to provide food or habitat that encourage deer. It's not about managing deer, their director said; it's about managing human behaviour – a statement heartily endorsed by the Conservation Authority and the Royal Botanical Gardens, who look after most of the conservation lands around Hamilton. They said humans

Daniel Coleman

are responsible for the deer problem and that the situation is a result of urban development – mostly roads, but other structures, too – that have pressed the deer into smaller and smaller places.

City planners in their suits and ties have mapped out neighbourhoods, highways and shopping centres without thinking about the deer, wearing their own coats, living in our midst. They thought that saving a few acres for parks would do the job. But instead of keeping these deer in tiny bits of wild where we could visit them on Sunday afternoons, the roads and subdivisions we built have packed them into a reproductive pressure cooker.

And creating these kinds of pressure cookers can have weird effects. Consider, for example, the mothballed US Army Depot in Seneca County, New York, just a little southwest of where Oren Lyons saw those two does and a yearling tiptoe into that suburb in Syracuse. Situated in the middle of the traditional territory where Generals Sullivan and Clinton burnt the Hodinöhsö:ni' out of their homes during the Revolutionary War, this massive leftover from the Cold War is made up of ten and a half thousand acres closed in by thirty-nine kilometres of fence. This is where the US Army stockpiled ammunition and dangerous explosives until the depot was decommissioned in the year 2000. Now, the site consists of housing for troubled youth, a maximum-security state prison and a medium-security reservation for about two hundred pure white, head-to-toe, white-tailed deer.

This freak colouring has to do with those thirty-nine kilometres of fence, because, like the tangle of highways around Iroquoia Heights, they have created an artificial reproductive island. In the 1940s, Colonel Franklin Kemble Jr., who was commander of the depot, learned that there were some white deer on the base. They weren't albinos with pink eyes. They had regular brown eyes and a naturally occurring, recessive gene that produces what is called leucism.

The stark white coats of these leucistic deer would make it difficult for them to survive in the wild. They would be too visible to predators and hunters. In addition, leucistic animals are prone to what scientists call inbreeding depression, which shows up in birth deformities, fewer pregnancies or unsuccessful births. Maybe it was for these reasons that Colonel Kemble Jr. had a soft spot for the leucistic deer. During his term as commander, the army allowed hunting every fall on the land inside that long fence, but he put out an order that nobody could shoot the white deer. The result is that regular brown deer got culled while the white deer increased in number. There are about two hundred of them now out of a total of eight hundred deer on the decommissioned depot.

Some call them ghost deer and link them to King Arthur's hunt for the white stag. Other people connect them to a prophecy that they say comes from the Lenape (or Delaware) people. According to this prophecy, when you see a white male and white female deer together, it's a sign for the people to gather as one.

Somehow, I don't think Oren Lyons was talking about deer in army-issued white coats when he said all life is equal and worthy of our respect. It would feel like pulling wires off stage in a magic show if the prophesied coming together were presaged by genetic engineering.

DOWN IN THE DEER yard, it's turned out that, alongside antlers, injuries are the easiest way for me to distinguish one family member from another. One Sunday afternoon, I watched one of the adult females for an hour and was able to get close enough to take some photographs, because she must have either broken or dislocated her right foreleg some time back. It joined her shoulder with an ugly crook – the kind you see when someone throws out their shoulder and you get that queasy feeling in your stomach looking at the slump by their neck where their shoulder should be. And the length of her tibia between her patella and her tarsal joint – if we were talking about a human leg, we would say between hip and knee – looked much shorter than on her healthy leg. I could see she didn't like to put weight on that leg. Mostly, she let it dangle, rarely touching the ground, as she grazed from grass to alder bark. I followed at a distance each time she moved. She'd hump her back and heave her good hoof forward, her head jerking up at the end of each hop. It was January in a strangely warm winter, but there were still cold months ahead, and I wondered how she would make it. If she would make it. When the snow got deep, would she be able to dig enough away to get something to eat? There were no ribs showing, so that seemed like a good thing. She looked plump enough to my inexperienced eye.

I checked in on her regularly over the rest of the winter. Thanks to the warm temperatures and little snowfall, she continued looking healthy, except for the limp. I startled her among her family once or twice when I came down to the yard, and when she ran, she seemed smoother and more sure-footed than when she walked. Somehow it's easier to perform that series of graceful, half-moon vaults on three legs than it is to walk. If she could run and vault, I guessed she had a chance against predators, if any still lived in the valley. I've seen single coyotes a few times in the valley, and a red fox or two. But I've never heard of foxes going after a deer, and coyotes are opportunists. They might try to take down an adult deer if they're in a pack, but on their own, they are more likely to scare up something small, like a rabbit or a field mouse. But who knows? There have been articles in the *Spectator* about the rising number of coyotes in the city's park system. So maybe there are enough to form a pack. I've never seen tracks of more than one coyote, but then again I don't know how to tell the difference between coyote and dog tracks. So I have no idea if the single sets I've seen are one or the other.

I wondered about predators when I got my first close look through binoculars at one of the twin fawns in the limping doe's clan. The first time I glimpsed him, I didn't have the field glasses. With my bare eyes, I saw one of the fawns had strange racing stripes, bright white, following the curve of his back haunches on both sides of his body. They looked like a deer version of those dramatic flames you see painted on the back fenders of a muscle car. But the next time I went down to the yard, I had a good look through the glasses and realized they weren't stripes, but scars.

Huge scars of raw meat, five inches across, almost identical on both sides of his body, right in front of the big round leg muscles on his back end. The little one's thick winter fur looked like it had been shaved back from the wounds, and I could see that what I had thought were racing stripes were the white edge lines where the shaggy winter coat had been sheared away. The wounds were not fresh, as the exposed flesh looked oxblood dry, like jerky.

What could have caused such stomach-churning scars? And why were they exactly the same on both sides?

Everywhere else, this fawn's fur looked thick and rich, so I didn't think he had mange, which wouldn't appear in exactly the same place on each side. Did some predator grab him from behind, claws tearing at both sides of his body, like lions do to wildebeests in *National Geographic*? But what animal would do that here in our ravine? A dog or coyote, back when this young deer was tiny? The scars didn't look like the raking motions of claws, though, so I didn't put much stock in this possibility. Or, how about this: Could the curious little guy have got stuck in a spot too narrow to pass through and jerked himself free, tearing both sides of his body at the hips? I think again of the full-grown doe who squeezed through the eight-inch gap between our fence and our neighbour's carport.

What violent or accidental story do these scars tell?

I started keeping an eye out, not just for Limping Doe, but also the one with the patches, all through the winter months. I worried that infection, plus the lack of a winter coat at his back end, would make him prone to sickness and cold. But each time I saw him over the next three months, I saw more and more fur covered those bald spots. During the spring moult in April, I had a moment when I wasn't sure if the young one with the mussed-up spots near its haunches was Scars or his sister. This time of year, all the deer have cowlicks of fur that stick up from their bodies like old roof shingles curling in the sun as they shed their winter hair, so it was difficult to tell what was scarring and what was moult.

By the next fall, I couldn't tell which was him and which his sister. But by then, they were starting to get big enough that I was also having difficulty distinguishing them from the does. And, I realized, the he with the scars was actually a she – she showed no signs of antler buds. I never did unearth a cause for her wounds, and she eventually healed so successfully, I lost the ability to distinguish her from the others in her clan.

DURING THE DEER DEBATES in the paper, Rick Hill sent in an article titled "The Role of Deer in Hodinöhsö:ni' Culture." He pointed out that "the deer were never meant to be in an urban reservation that you call a park. They are meant to have this range. Our job is to help maintain this natural intended balance." Sounding a lot like Oren Lyons, Hill goes on to say that for Six Nations people, hunting deer isn't recreation or sport. It's ceremonial. He says venison is spirit food, part of the yearly cycle. For centuries, men have brought it home from the woods and exchanged it for cornbread grown and made by women. The meat and hide play a big part in the Midwinter Ceremonies that involve rituals of thanksgiving for Creation's generosity. "When we gather in our community," Hill says, "we always give thanks to the deer and animals that provide this for us as well as the foods. You could say it's right at the heart of the culture."

The story of the twin brothers connects deer to the good mind and the idea of protecting creation's goodness. I don't know if the Deer Management Advisory Committee were convinced by the idea of the good mind, or if they were more strategic and saw in it a window to let fresh air into a fetid debate, but they eventually adopted what we might call the Hodinöhsö:ni' solution. For the past five Decembers, signs and yellow caution tape have been

posted at trailheads, and announcements have appeared in the
paper announcing that a large section of Hamilton's park system
has been closed from Mondays to Thursdays for a couple of weeks
while Six Nations bow hunters cull the deer in our city. The timing follows the usual deer hunting season, around the period of
the fall rut, and it comes long enough before the Midwinter
Ceremonies that the men have time to do the butchering and
freezing before they exchange venison for the women's cornbread.

The deer have pretty much forced this issue, so that we humans have to recalibrate our relationships – not just with other
human beings, but also with the lands and creatures that make
up our neighbourhoods. We still think in roundabout, peekaboo
language, like "deer management." But we've been given a poke,
reminded, for the moment at least, of a long-ignored presence
among us. We have to readjust our assumptions, develop new
ways of thinking, maybe even open ourselves to a good mind.
Who knows? Maybe we'll become better neighbours, get better at
living with ourselves, because the deer, wearing their own coats,
pushed into our notice.

I WONDER IF BUCKS' heads get itchy when they are losing their
antlers. I can imagine it might get irritating when the new antlers
start to push at the roots of the old ones, like adult teeth pushing
out baby ones.

Whatever it feels like for them, antlers have had me scratching my own head. I saw a picture of an antler lying in a bed of dry
leaves that someone sent in to the newspaper during the Iroquoia

Heights kerfuffle. It made me think, I'd love to come across a set myself. Having it would remind me to side with my good mind, and to see through the temptations of my restless, jealous one.

So isn't it more than a little significant that after months of looking, I finally found an antler, and not just on any day but on Easter Sunday? I'd been reminded how religiously and culturally packed Easter weekend is by attending a Passover Seder at a friend's house. The Seder is a long, ceremonial meal during which Jews and their dinner guests eat bitter herbs to remind them of the bitterness of slavery. They dip these herbs in salt to remind themselves of the grief of having to flee their homes, and they chew on matzo bread to remember that the escaping slaves didn't have time to let bread rise when they fled. This super-significant weekend layers the Jewish story of liberation from slavery with the Christian story of Jesus rising up out of the earth and giving everyone new life. Passover is set in the Hebrew month of Nisan, at the end of winter and the beginning of a new growing season. So both the Christian and Jewish ceremonies are layered over older spring-fertility rites, which, like the Midwinter Ceremonies, celebrate nature's yearly cycle of death and rebirth.

On this particular Easter Sunday, I woke before dawn, made a thermos of coffee, zipped up my winter coat, grabbed my hat and gloves and stepped out into the frosty April morning. Thinking of all the layers of meaning attached to this particular morning, I burned some sweet grass, watching the smoke rise into the grey morning air, and said the lines of an Anishnaabe prayer translated by Basil Johnston:

By you, Father
Through the sun
You work your powers
To dispel the night
Bring day anew
A new life, a new time.

To you, Father
Through the sun
We give thanks
For your light
For your warmth
That gives light to all.

I then walked over to the Marks Binkley Cemetery to pay my respects to the people in the ground. Also, the cemetery has a high, east-facing slope. There, I could watch the sun lift through the trees. I stood there with Marks and Mathelena to watch the new sun rise.

Waves of cloud licked at the horizon: pink, peach, then gold. Movement caught my eye in the grey leaf-litter on the forest floor down in the ravine below. I watched while four shadowy figures emerged from the gloom. One had a distinct limp. Limping Doe, the one with the scars, her sister and a sure-footed auntie I've also seen many times.

I slid the glasses from my coat pocket, silent as possible. But my tiny movements were still big enough to perk their ears. The full beam of four pairs of deer radar glowed up the gully at me. They hesitated on the path leading up the slope thirty metres from where I was standing. They milled about, uncertain of whether or not to proceed. Always the curious one, Scars stepped from the group and, one hoof at a time, began a careful, gradual climb – stop and scent, step and pause – up the slope toward me. All the while, she kept me in her steady gaze, her breath steaming the air.

As she walked toward me, I got a good look at her wounds. They were definitely healing: the patch on her left side was now completely covered in fur. A faint outline was all that was left of the racing stripes of white under-fur near her haunch. You'd only know to look for it if you knew what had once been there. The bald leathery patch on her right side had shrunk from seven to three inches across. There were no signs of the dried red I had seen six weeks ago.

Limping Doe's condition, however, remained the same, her walk halting as ever. Finally, she overcame her nervousness about me being here and took a couple of graceful round vaults up the slope and onto the lawn by the entrance to the cemetery. Her gait was still smoother when she bounded than when she walked.

After their clan passed, I followed them to the deer yard farther down the valley to see who else might be there this morning. I'd wondered how the doe and bachelor groups interacted when they met up, especially now that mating season was long over.

When they realized that I was following thirty metres back, the family waved their white flags at me and trotted, ears perked, down into the marshy yard that used to be Binkley's Pond. Expecting to see them spread out and settled, tugging with their teeth at the tufts of new green starting to emerge from the mud and water, I was surprised, when I peered over the lip of the bowl, to see a buck with two rust-coloured, furry bumps where his antlers used to be, chewing and gazing at me steadily. To his left I saw another deer, and when I adjusted the focus on the binoculars, I saw that he, too, had antler bumps, black this time, leather-looking and swollen. Farther left, I caught more movement and panned the binoculars to find another buck, also in bud. I watched these three from the rim of the yard for fifteen minutes, swivelling the binoculars from one to the next. Then, a flick of an ear close to the ground alerted me to a fourth, lying down and chewing his cud behind a tangle of wild grape – this one, like the first, with those reddish, furry buds. A bachelor group. I had seen a solitary buck ten days earlier, but hadn't seen bucks together for at least three months, maybe four.

A flick of movement fifty metres to the left of these guys turned out to be Limping Doe and her group feeding on the marsh grass farther along in the yard. They must have come down the trail I was standing on and skirted around the four bachelors. As I turned my eyes back across the yard, looking from the doe group to the bachelors, I glimpsed an odd forma-tion low down on the trunk of a skinny black walnut. All the limbs had broken off along the lower section of the tree, leaving this strangely shaped branch by itself. There was no reason why such an old, dried branch would not also have snapped off. But more than this, it was too big for the six-inch diameter of the trunk. And why would it be bare, polished clean of bark, when the tree trunk's rough skin was still intact?

Then it dawned on me.

I excitedly raised my binoculars and twiddled the focus. Sure enough! It wasn't a branch. Points embedded in the bark, three feet up from the ground: an antler.

An offering. A blessing.

I'd been telling myself not to hope to find antlers. It was too cheesy, too wannabe native, too symbolic. But I'd hoped nonetheless. If it by thy will. This is the kind of thing you don't demand, though I knew the chances of it happening were higher if I showed up.

I guess I'd been showing up.

Not hidden in a tangle of grape vines. Not lost among the boneyard of dead branches scattered all over the floor of the deer yard. The antler was actually hanging from a tree, just as Creator Brother hung deer antlers high to mark the area for the good mind, and what was off limits for the troubled one.

It's easy to get misty eyed when you find a deer's crown hanging on a tree on Easter Sunday morning. Hard not to think of Passover lambs sacrificed to save innocent children from the Angel of Death, of Jesus's crown of thorns, of antlers given to help the Creator win the battle against the jealous mind.

What was this antler doing here? Was this the result of a scrape, as the buck added tree bark to his musk-and-urine rub? Does the itch of the growing antlers make bucks rub their antlers against trees to try and knock them off?

Later, I read that black walnut is rich in a compound called juglone, which is so toxic that many plants can't grow in its vicinity. But the deer know it's also a good blood-clotting agent, and they rub their antlers on walnut trees, hoping to scar the tree and release the juglone. And when the irritating antler finally comes off, they've got the agent they need right there for the bleeding pedicle that remains where the old rack had been attached.

Whatever the reason, the deer hung his antler up on a tree in a place where I could see it easily. I'd walked through this part of the yard time and again for weeks, aware that the bucks would have dropped antlers over the past months. I'd scanned the ground, poked among the boneyard of branches, surveyed the compost of the marsh where the skunk cabbages were about to unroll wide umbrella leaves, peered deep into the tangles of grape and wild rose. Never seen a thing.

I couldn't get it out of my mind that it was on Easter morning, of all mornings, that one of these bucks in the bachelor group behind me hung an antler high enough for me to see. It was as if he were saying, "I know this is a big day in your religion."

I felt like falling to my knees.

Instead, I teetered across a fallen log over a marshy spot steaming with deer rub. I stepped down from the log and crossed the new grass and old leaves to the walnut to have a look at the hanging antler. It had three points now; used to have four. The one closest to the skull must have broken off a while back. I could tell because the jagged edges where it broke had been smoothed and stained with time. The next tine up, the longest, was jammed into a gash in the tree bark about five inches long. The middle tine was impaled in the bark with no gash line above or below it. The last tine, farthest from the head, stuck out into mid-air, pointing back the way I had come. I was thinking the first tine must have been dragged down the tree trunk, and when the middle tine hit the bark, the base of the antler snapped off.

Free deer. Free gift.

I lifted the antler away from the marks on the tree. It came away easily – too easily to have been here very long. A good wind or rainstorm would have knocked it down. The marks in the tree bark didn't look especially fresh, either. So there wouldn't be fresh wood inside to expose. Had the antler been here for days? Or did one of these bachelors hang it up here this morning? Hard to tell.

I turned toward the four bucks, who were still grazing the fresh leaves uncurling on the highbush cranberries.

I bowed from the waist, antler in hand.

I watched them for a minute.

I bowed from the waist again: thank you.

So far the bucks had kept me in sight, but they hadn't given me much notice as they continued to crop new grass. Now one stepped toward me, ears perked high, black eyes alert, nose quivering.

He bowed, too. Down. Then up.

Stamped his hoof. Thump. It was louder than the yearling's stamp in the winter. Louder now that the snow was gone.

He bowed again. Down. Then up.

His eyes, wide open, deep and black, gazed into mine.

Then he startled us all with a sharp huff of air, blown through his nostrils. The others trotted back a few paces.

The doe group lifted their heads and looked at us from across the yard.

So I turned to them and bowed again. Down. Then up.

Backyard, northeast corner

Traffic

HUNKERING DOWN IN ONE place and giving my attention to one backyard might seem a narrow thing to do. By drawing a line around this one little spot, I could appear to rule out the rest of the planet – a version of burying my head in the sand, or focusing all my attention on my intimate circle and saying the rest of the world can go to hell.

Strangely, however, I have found that the more I focus in, the bigger this place grows. It wasn't long before it dawned on me that this tiny patch of earth is a major hub: a meeting point of deer paths, canoe portages, vapour trails and sailing itineraries. So many have passed – are still passing – through here, from Princess Point people and the Attawandaron to Michi Saagiig and Jesuit priests, from white pines and black walnuts to euonymus and cedar hedges, and from groundhogs and raccoons to English sparrows and northern red cardinals. From air to sky to water and tunnels underground, this place is a node in a global network.

Each movement in this network generates movement in another part. I encountered this mobile interconnectedness when we had to take down the chokecherry tree in our neighbour's yard that used to lean way over our euonymus hedge. One problem was that, as it grew taller, it teetered more and more precariously over our garden and stippled our roof with round, purple, pea-sized berries. I worried that during some winter ice storm, the heavy, leaning top might break off and fall on our sunroom. A second problem was that its branches produced clusters of berries in the late summer, and pelted everything with them, little purple ball bearings that gathered in mounds everywhere: roof, eavestroughs, sidewalks, back steps, garden beds. They were small as wild blueberries and hard as peppercorns. They roll under a person's shoe, and more than once I was on my backside before I knew it. They're scentless, hard and dry, and maybe that's why nobody ate them. When I looked them up, I was puzzled to learn that the fruits of most cherries, even pin cherries and chokecherries, are supposed to be attractive to birds. Not these hard and bitter little pellets. Every July, the birds, squirrels and raccoons crowd into the Bing cherry tree in our other neighbour's yard and gorge themselves on its sweet fruit. But unlike their winsome cousins, these bitter cherries would hang undisturbed until they were ready to drop. Then they dropped like hail, bouncing down and collecting in drifts. I expected that, being so dry, they'd have no colour left, but rain could still leach enough purple out of them to leave dark bruises on our steps and sidewalks. And they could still germinate, too, because every spring, we had buckets full of baby chokecherry trees to weed out of the garden.

This past winter, when the garden plants were still napping, we hired a crew to take down the chokecherry. The tree guys had the whole thing down – the branches in the chipper and the heavier chunks carted away – in half a day. Standing in the February sunshine with the smell of fresh sawdust rising from the bright snow, I counted forty-three tree rings in the smooth cut. Forty-three years of growth – of seeking the sun, of dropping cartloads of leaves in the fall and budding new ones in the spring, of carrying ground water up to the light – gone in three hours. Our neighbour's son has a lumber mill and was happy to keep the straightest part of the trunk to make cherry one-by-sixes. For us, it was a relief to see the messy thing go.

But even a seasonally irritating chokecherry that threatens your home and drops ball bearings all over the place reminds you everything is connected.

The former cherry's side of the garden is jammed with plants that we selected for mixed sun and shade. And now we've subtracted most of the shade, which means that when the growing season gets started, we'll have to see how they get along with more direct and intense sunlight.

We also hadn't thought about the squirrels.

If anybody treats our yard as a junction of superhighways, it would be squirrels. I would love to see a squirrel map of this neighbourhood, which would have to be three-dimensional, because they have so many vertical layers in their system of roads, overpasses and bridges. When we took down the chokecherry, it was as if we had closed the Skyway Bridge on the QEW Highway between Toronto and Niagara.

Grey, black and red squirrels make up the major traffic here. The grey and black ones are the same size as each other and twice as big as the reds. Nonetheless, nine times out of ten, I will see a little red blur blazing along a branch, chasing off a harried but half-amused grey or black. These bigger squirrels know they're brawnier than the puny red that's chasing them, but they still don't trust how enraged that red is. It's like seeing a kid in a sports car weaving in and out of the HOV lane: a driver never knows how much damage they could do.

The American red is hyper-territorial. Each mother claims a radius of one hundred fifty metres and shoots out chittering after anything – I mean *anything* – that might possibly trespass on her private stash of pine, spruce and other cones. I've seen red squirrels buzz robins and dogs as readily as humans and raccoons. The reds are exclusively conifer eaters, unlike blacks and greys who aren't as picky in their diets. Reds stake out their own territory, acting like trolls under the bridge, always in a fury at passing traffic. This fury seems to occupy about half their day, because there is never a moment in this yard that's free of traffic.

Talking about blacks and greys and reds might make you think they are all different kinds of squirrels. Not so. Reds are a different species, but the blacks and greys are together known as eastern grey squirrels. All eastern greys share the same body shape, which are surprisingly rabbit- or kangaroo-like, with muscular back legs and haunches that propel their remarkable jumping capacities, and small shoulders and front paws that give them manual dexterity. Their fur colour varies, however, and the difference is especially noticeable in the wispy tails of the black ones as compared to the greys' luxuriant, thick boas, fashionably frosted at the end of each hair with a white tip. The black squirrels constitute what scientists call a melanistic subgroup.

The gestation of eastern grey squirrels is forty-four days, and black babies result if they have at least one or two of what one website calls "mutant pigment genes." Language like this makes me wonder how grey became the norm and black mutant? The eastern grey squirrel's traditional range was from Florida to here and their western limit was Minnesota. However, with the spread of squirrel-friendly cities around the whole continent, they are now regular residents today in Seattle and Vancouver. So this species has travelled with humans from coast to coast, some-times in cages, but mostly moving from tree to tree. They were first observed by record-keeping Europeans in the Carolinas. In southern Ontario, we have as many or more black squirrels as greys. If the record-keeping people had arrived first in Upper Canada instead of Carolina, might they have called them eastern black squirrels, and the greys would have been known as melanin-challenged mutants?

Blacks and greys might not be wound as tightly as reds, but no squirrel is by nature relaxed. Everything with them is full on and high-speed. When one scratches behind its ear with a hind foot or turns its head to check out a sound, it becomes cartoon-like, reminding me of the times when Wile E. Coyote's foot looks more like a wheel or a motor than a foot. A twig snaps, and they've already turned toward the sound before I hear it myself. To live like they do, they've got to have lightning reflexes. A person sprinting from branch to twig to fence post to roof top at fifty kilometres an hour would have to have nanosecond response times.

Maybe their sped-up ways come from high sugar content in their diet. Most people know squirrels save nuts and acorns for winter, but they eat all kinds of things. The Royal Botanical Gardens plants its masses of tulip bulbs under chicken-wire fencing buried in the ground to keep the squirrels from digging up the spring displays. In her book on forest ecology, Diana Beresford-Kroeger says squirrels will find a tree with sweet sap and strip away a bit of bark to get down to the cambium layer where the tree's fluids flow through the xylem and phloem tubes. In winter, this scar will leak a sugary popsicle, which the squirrels feast upon. Chickadees and other winter birds will come along for a sip, too. These wily squirrels tap trees for high-octane fuel.

Now that we've taken down the chokecherry, though, the squirrels have to update their neighbourhood map. They used to shoot from the juglone-bearing black walnut west of our place to that pinosylvin-breathing young white pine, from it to the vitamin-rich cedar tree at the end of our hedge and then to the broken pine. The easternmost branch of the broken pine on that western side of the yard used to touch the westernmost branch of the unbroken pine on the eastern side. Squirrel traffic would streak right across. But over the years, with the breaking nature of pine trees, wind and ice have taken out the bridge, piece by piece, branch by branch, and nobody thought to close the on-ramps. Now, the reds, blacks and greys speed out on the broken pine and skid to a halt when they see how far they have to jump to get to the eastern side. The closest branch from this side has had bits break off of it, as well, and what remains is more of a twig than a branch. Not only is it a six-foot jump, but it's also a four-foot drop onto a twig that doesn't look solid at all.

The little red fireballs hardly notice. They're so small that they shoot across the gap and barely dip the lower twig when they land on it. But lots of blacks and greys hesitate, and turn around and look at it, and turn again and think about it, like a ten-year-old on a high dive board. Some decide to back up and take the leap. When they do, their bulk causes them to slip around under the twig upon landing, and they have to scramble to right themselves as the branch bobs up and down under the shock of their weight. Others back off and skitter down the tree trunk, suffering the indignity – and danger – of travelling on the ground. Tall ferns and false Solomon's seal grow around the base of those pines and stealthy neighbourhood cats like to hide under their cover.

But many squirrels take the dare. I once saw a grey take the kamikaze leap and miss the twig. He dropped twenty-five feet to the ground. I couldn't believe what I was seeing – squirrels never miss, do they? I ran down to see if he was okay, but by the time I got there, he had already scrambled up the opposite pine and was chattering and whipping his tail at me, at the world, at the fault of things.

When we took down the cherry, we threw a monkey wrench in the local works. Where the squirrels used to leap from the un-broken pine onto the cherry and from there to our neighbour's cedars in the east, they now have to go the long way around. Sometimes, they pick the dense and scratchy euonymus hedge that grows down our fenceline, a route that is pretty slow going for a squirrel. Other times, they jump from the unbroken pine to the softwood maple down the slope behind the pine, then to the Manitoba maple above and then to the cedars – a good fifty metres farther around than the old route via the cherry.

In squirrel time, that's forever – which means that I rarely see the red ones blazing after blacks and greys at that end of the yard anymore. Removing the tree must have changed the terri-tory borders. I still see reds raging at the bigger squirrels on the west side of our yard, but not so much on this side.

I didn't learn until months after taking down this tree that some longhouse people have suggested that the Tree of Lights, Hodä:he', and his wife, Atsi'tsiaká:ion, uprooted in the Sky World may have been a wild cherry. Perhaps she slipped on the ball bearings produced by the cherry and fell through the hole after its roots had been torn out of the ground. Or maybe its spears of white blossoms that glow bright as candles reminded people of the lights in the original sacred tree. All I know is that the peppercorn-dropping, dangerously tilted chokecherry tree in our yard, like anything else in nature, was a linchpin holding together a whole system of living things. Just as happened when they uprooted the Tree of Lights, pulling that pin causes a whole interlocking set of lives – from plants to animals to humans – to reset and restart.

IF SQUIRRELS DRAW OUR attention to an aerial traffic map, insects add a subterranean dimension to it. Take for example the dog-day cicada I found resting on the step when I opened the backdoor one summer day. People call the cicadas we have around here dog-day cicadas because they produce a shimmering whine that emanates from high up in the trees on the hottest, muggiest days of July and August. These are the dog days, when the bright Dog Star, known by Greeks as Sirius or by Romans as Alpha Canis Major, rises and sets with the sun. Until this cicada ended up on our back step, I'd never noticed how their wings are composed of outlined sections, like stained glass, except that theirs is clear, not coloured. Stock still on the back step, the cicada's green and black camouflage body looked like a two-inch bullet parked in its own little glass house – a blunt, six-legged turtle in a clear shell.

Adult cicadas live two to five years up in the trees. I'd never seen one before, but I know where they are because I've heard them singing and buzzing in the chokecherry, as well as the pines and maples around the yard. The females jam their clusters of eggs into crevices in the bark of twigs and small branches. Nymphs hatch from the eggs and drop to the ground after six or seven weeks. These newborns dig into the soil, looking for the sap of tree roots, their favourite food. David George Haskell calls them moles with syringes. They remind me of other root-tappers, the white grubs who eat my grass roots from underneath. They literally bury their heads, and then their whole bodies, in the sand to get to the sugary sap.

All plants have teeth and pincers sawing at them from above and below. Or to consider it from the opposite point of view, any plant you see is feeding a whole galaxy of living, crawling beings. There's a complex living, eating, syringing universe going on in that subterranean domain.

These cicada nymphs moult underground as they progress through a series of growth stages. First, they dig down several feet and tap root sap. Then, at a certain stage of maturity, they dig their way back up to the surface, always at night, emerging from what look like cones or chimneys of mud as tall as three to four inches in height.

Next, these nymphs scramble up tree trunks, plants, or other objects – anything pointing up, such as the latticework screen behind our smaller patio. Once they get somewhere high, their skin cracks along the back and the adults climb out, leaving an exact model of themselves behind. The empty case I found on the lattice made me think at first it was a living cicada, frozen stock still as it climbed the wood post. Then I looked closer and realized there wasn't anybody inside.

That feverish buzz coming from the trees on summer dog days, when everyone is sticky and irritable, is the sound of adult males shouting their desire for a mate. I've wanted to see how they make that racket, but despite scanning my trees with binoculars when I hear them, I can never pinpoint exactly where it's coming from. It is as if they are ventriloquists, throwing their voices all over the yard. Haskell writes that the males have a row of discs embedded on each side of the hard shell of their thorax. Each disc consists of a membrane stretched across an air-filled sack. On each side of the body, the row of discs looks like a line of tiny portholes with bars in each one, and these tiny bars snap back and forth when a muscle pulls on the disc. When the male cicada wants to call females, it shimmies the muscles in its thorax, causing the bars in the rows of discs to cascade like a drum roll, and the sound gets magnified by the hollow sack underneath. Cicadas do this cascading shimmy like a motor, at a rate of 7,400 pulses per minute. It can be so loud that people have heard it from well over a mile away.

We have basic cicadas here in Hamilton, not the periodical variety expected to hatch this year in the billions in a number of eastern states, including New York. Periodical cicadas are different from annual or dog-day cicadas, because the periodicals stay underground as juveniles for incredibly long periods – some for thirteen and others for seventeen years! Then they boil out of their chimneys in hordes when the thermometer gets to exactly eighteen degrees Celsius. On the magic spring night when the mercury rises to eighteen, entomologists have counted as many as one and a half million cicadas climbing out of *one acre of ground*. I've seen TV images of a night when several billion emerged in upstate New York – so many that cars slipped off the roads on their grease. For some reason unknown to me, even this close by, with just the Niagara River in between, we don't have the periodical cicadas that are so temperature- and calendar-driven. Here at the Head-of-the-Lake, each nymph has its own timing, and any given year some are being born up in the trees while others are climbing out of their dirt chimneys.

Whether dog-day or periodical, the life cycle of the cicada is a journey up the height and down the depth of trees – a sort of vertical migration, from the mysterious underground that we can never see to the upper world of sunlight and tree tops, where birds and pollen and leaves blow in the breeze. There are three thousand species of cicadas worldwide, so when I look at that one dog-day cicada resting on my back step, I'm looking at a member of a huge, spread-out family, a diaspora of insects who live this up-and-down-the-trees life. And it's not stretching things to say that this one knows and has poked his blunt head into parts of my backyard that I have never seen and know very little about.

Cicadas are just one of the millions of kinds of bugs that track and trail across and through this little eighteen-by-thirty-six-metre plot of ground. Others, like monarch butterflies, pass through here on their yearly trip from Mexico to Hudson Bay and beyond, despite their being made of what looks like no more than single-ply tissue. The bug I see on my back step may have settled on one little patch of ground in one small city on the curve of one lake in North America, but the traffic and business it's a part of, in this one patch and beyond, is immense. If I decided to try and keep track of every living thing that wanders around this one yard, from those who live off grass and tree roots to those who fly through the air, I would need Google headquarters to store the list. If I roped off just one square metre, as David Haskell did in the Tennessee woods, and noted all that skitters and wriggles through it, plus where they have been, I would be tracking dimensions and destinations for the rest of my life.

SOME BACKYARD TRAFFIC IS dramatic and visible, like high-speed squirrel traffic, while other traffic is hidden, like tree-root-sipping cicada nymphs. Most people would put bird traffic in the former group. Their yearly migrations are surely dramatic and eye-catching, such as the clouds of starlings that roil through the air in autumn or the long Vs of geese that honk overhead.

Take that hummingbird helicoptering between our feeder and the coralbells. Its body is so small that more than once I've looked up to see what I thought at first was a large bumblebee and realized, *No, that's a bird.* The speed of its wingbeats makes it a blur in the air – a hazy, moving asterisk.

Hummingbirds like the three-inch, ruby-throated ones that frequent our place are commonplace in an Ontario city garden. But their resumé contains one unbelievable feat after another. To hover as they do, stock still as they poke their long beaks into the mouth of a trumpet flower, the average-sized ones beat their wings up to eighty times per second. And their tiny hearts can beat twenty-one times a second. If you put a stethoscope to a hummingbird's chest, what would you hear? Perhaps a purr? Or the whine of a quiet cicada?

To maintain this high performance, hummingbirds drink hundreds of flowers every day. They suck in more than their body weight in nectar every twenty-four hours. Contrary to popular opinion, this exquisite sugary diet is not their primary source of food. The sugar gives them energy to hunt bugs and spiders, their main sustenance. If they don't get enough nectar, they can't chase bugs, and they die. A heart rate of twelve hundred beats a minute requires extremely high voltage.

Hummingbirds can't feed all night though, so they have a nighttime, cool weather hibernator built right into their bodies. On chilly nights, they withdraw into a state called "torpor," slowing their heart rate down to between fifty and a hundred-and-eighty beats per minute. Then, when the sun rises and things warm up again the next day, they rev back up to twelve hundred beats and go looking for sugar and bugs.

I'm watching as one of these bits of feathered intensity blurs over my coralbells when it hits me: this creature the size of a moth flies every spring and fall four to five thousand kilometres between here and Central America! It's the length of my pinkie finger, yet it has navigated the skies and flowers of Ohio, Kentucky, Missouri, Arkansas, Texas, Mexico, Guatemala, Honduras and Nicaragua on its way to its winter hovering grounds in Costa Rica or Panama. Or, if it's among the radicals of its kind, it skips the overland route and makes the twenty-some-hour, non-stop flight across the Gulf of Mexico from the Texas coast to a destination like Colón, Panama, or Limón, Costa Rica.

These facts are like a sharp elbow to the ribs: show some respect! This dandelion fluff of a bird that I'm watching on a warm June day has hovered at someone's feeder in Texas in February and over the bushy, red *cepillo* flowers in Costa Rica in December. And it's going to make the return trip in a month or so, as soon as its young are ready. This speck of sugar and feathers knows all about head winds on the Gulf, particulate toxins in the air over Cincinnati, tornado conditions in Tennessee and how the number of smog days has changed here in Hamilton.

It knows this by comparison with what its ancestors have experienced in Costa Rica over the past forty years – a Central American country with one of the most forward-looking environmental programs in the world. Back in the 1970s, the rainforests there had been decimated to make room for massive cattle ranches. But without the tree cover, conditions turned out to be far from ideal, and the mega-ranch owners didn't achieve their desired quota of beef. So they packed up and quit the place, leaving both the economy and the ecology devastated. The Costa Ricans decided to get serious about restoring one by first restoring the other: the government put everything that used to go into military spending into paying farmers to help bring back the environment.

Talk about trusting the ground on which you live and rest, and how it can be a pillow of peace. Maybe we could try this in Canada!

By rerouting the military budget, the Costa Ricans were able to establish a Payment for Environmental Services program, allowing farmers to receive about one hundred sixty dollars US per acre to farm in a way that protects freshwater systems, biodiversity and forests that consume and reduce greenhouse gases. They have been so successful that half the country is covered in jungle again. The US has signed a debt-for-nature deal with Costa Rica that has forgiven two Costa Rican loan payments of fifty-six million dollars each in return for the jungles' absorption of American carbon emissions.

The hummingbirds at our feeder have been there and seen the results. They know what fresh oxygenated air tastes like. They have seen the increase in numbers of cepillo flowers, the jump in spiders and bugs to eat. They've seen their own numbers increase, since more of them survive the trip back north after beefing up – if you can call it that – in a healthier south. And they bring back the promise of how things could be in Hamilton's economy and politics.

BUT NOT ALL OF the birds who stop here are migrants that fly to Costa Rica for the winter. We also get migrants who come *here* for the winter. The soggy days of rain and slush that we get between November and February are apparently warm winter retreats for the slate-coloured juncos who show up around here during our cold season.

I was sitting out in the yard one October day last year, when I heard a muted "chit" close to the ground. I looked up, knowing it was a familiar voice that I hadn't heard for some time – long enough to have forgotten whose it was. There, hopping around the base of the yellowing coneflower stems were five or six slate-coloured juncos. They're back! I felt a ridiculous thrill at seeing them again.

Juncos tend to poke around on the ground in small gangs of six or ten, picking up seeds and spurting into the low branches of a bush at some secret signal. The males have dark, charcoal-coloured heads and, like many birds, their undercarriages are whitish, but otherwise they're evenly grey – a handsome shade of pencil lead. I don't know what it is about juncos, but each fall they give me a lift. Maybe it's their humble, seed-gathering, sociable habits. Many birds have big public voices that make territorial announcements to mates or enemies. But I've never heard a junco make a public announcement – at least not around here in winter. They use small, private voices to give pointers and tips to their fellow seed collectors. I've rarely seen a junco high in a tree like one of those sports car–red northern cardinals. These little ones are happy on the lower rungs. A lot of times, I don't really notice them, until a two-toothed smile catches my eye when they flip into the hedge. Next time I watch more closely, and I realize the two outside white feathers of their slate tails are hidden until they fly, like the way white-tailed deer lift that white flag when they run.

These little birds commute here from Hudson Bay and the Arctic beyond, two thousand kilometres or so. They breed in the north in summer and come south for our sloppy winters. Some go much farther south, right down to the borders of Florida in the east and Mexico in the west. But these ones, the ones that hang around here, seem to think that Hamilton at the Head-of-the-Lake is far enough. The migration map in my *Peterson Field Guide to Birds of North America* says they breed here. I've never seen a junco in our area during the summer breeding season. Maybe that's why they're so quiet and companionable when they come here in winter. If they were defending nests and young, they might be testier.

I looked up juncos in Robert Curry's *Birds of Hamilton and Surrounding Areas*. Published in 2006 by the Hamilton Naturalists' Club, it provides a level of local information you could never get in a general guide about birds of North America. Each bird is allotted a whole page describing the record number seen in one sighting, if and where they migrate, when they arrive and when they depart, whether bones of this particular bird have been found in nearby archaeological digs and a catalogue of sightings: where, when and how many.

The thing I like best about this book is that the author keeps track of the sightings listed by birdwatchers in this area all the way back to the nineteenth century. For instance, he records that "Thomas McIlwraith (1860) described the 'Common Snow Bird' as a common resident'; by 1894, he stated the 'Slate-Colored Junco' bred commonly throughout the country." Then Curry will note: "By contrast, George North did not find the junco nesting in the HSA [Hamilton Study Area] any time from the beginning of his birding in 1925 until 1956. On 17 June 1956, North, Huber Moore and Harvey Williams observed two territorial pairs along the Niagara Escarpment at Dublin Line, northwest of Milton."

You've got to admire the love in lines like these. The sentences are not dramatic, not an ornithological bodice-ripper or an opera, but there's more than a lifetime of passion in sentences like these. I read devotion in the sheer labour of keeping track, of listing different names applied to the same bird over the centuries, of writing it all down and passing it wholesale to the next generation of birders. Bob Curry cut his birding teeth tramping around this area with George North in the 1950s and '60s. George North collected what he knew from people like Minnie Graham, Carl Nunn, Ruby Mills and Robert Owen Merriman in the 1920s and '30s. Merriman picked up his bird knowledge from records kept by Allan Cyril Brooks, who studied with Thomas McIlwraith in the 1880s. The history of the Hamilton Naturalists' Club, which

evolved out of what had been formerly called the Bird Protection
Society, represents nearly seven generations of people throughout our area who have cared about and for the lives of local birds
and the ecologies in which they live.

It is also eye-opening to watch the bird statistics over time in
Curry's book. Thomas McIlwraith knew birds. He was not likely
to be wrong about juncos nesting here in the 1860s. So what happened? Why were none nesting in the vicinity anymore in the
1920s, when George North started keeping track? Were there
extra-cold decades in the late nineteenth century? Was it that
these slate-grey birds couldn't survive around Hudson Bay, so
they stayed here in the south to lay their eggs? Did incoming rivals
such as English sparrows chase them up north for the summers?

We call house sparrows *English* because they are literally from
England. For some hard-to-imagine reason, people in the nineteenth century thought North America needed a new variety of
sparrow, despite there being thirty-some kinds of sparrows already
on the continent. So the directors of the Brooklyn Institute in
New York City imported the first eight pairs of English sparrows
in 1850. It became a kind of craze to bring sparrows from Britain.
Thomas McIlwraith described the arrival of the first house sparrows in Gore Park, Hamilton, in 1875. A birdhouse and feeder
had been set up. "But the sparrows, unused to so much kind-
ness, seemed afraid that there was some trap about the house,
or poison in the food, and betook themselves to the road tracks
for food, and found nesting-places of their own choice." At first,
McIlwraith joined the craze and set up a house and feeder of his
own, but fairly soon he noticed that the English imports were
pushing tree swallows from their nest boxes and eating his grape

buds. It wasn't long before he was shooting them. By the end of the century, the craze had switched from love to hatred, and people were organizing shooting sprees targeting English sparrows. Curry tells of a note in the *Brampton Conservator* of February 28, 1902, reporting on a sparrow-shooting contest that month in Streetsville, fifty kilometres north and a little east of Hamilton. The winners entertained the losers at the Royal Hotel with an oyster supper, celebrating the shooting deaths of three thousand sparrows.

Wayne Grady, who writes about animal life in Toronto, says that bringing in house sparrows pushed out native birds. One of the main losers was the eastern bluebird, which he says used to be as numerous in this region as the sparrow and is now listed as rare. He names other local birds that gave way to the sparrows, but he doesn't mention juncos. Maybe they're too small and grey to draw the kind of notice a bluebird does. Perhaps the fact that they still quietly arrive here for the winters in good numbers disqualifies them as a poster child for displaced species.

Whatever the reason, they used to raise their young here and now they don't. Curry doesn't speculate about why. But when you read through his record of what happened over a hundred and fifty years, you see that junco traffic has changed over time. The continuity, the sharing of these records, is essential: if people didn't pass on their bird lists from one generation to the next, we'd lose significant muscle for tracking how much the ecosystem itself has changed over time.

TAKE CARDINALS AS ANOTHER example: compared to juncos and hummingbirds, northern cardinals are homebodies and don't fly to exotic destinations. They stick around, summer and winter, regular as rain – except they're too strikingly costumed to be thought of as regular. With their scarlet feather coats, square black masks and chunky red beaks, the males are the glamour gods of the backyard. The females have the same red beaks and some red racing stripes in their wing feathers, but they're mostly brown, which keeps them hidden while they're sitting on eggs. In winter, the males' red finery stands out against the snow. They're a Christmas card during those months when everything besides the snow is grey, brown and beige. A dozen juncos might be picking through the seeds under the euonymus hedge, all nice and friendly, but if so much as one cardinal hops up on a bare tree branch – as cardinals do in late winter – and whistles out its "birdy birdy birdy," it's hard to remember the juncos even exist.

Curry's book lists northern cardinals as "abundant, ubiquitous, permanent residents." But looking back over the hundred and fifty years of birdwatching in these parts, Curry notes that it wasn't always so. In the early nineteenth century, cardinals didn't live in this region. The first one recorded in southern Ontario was seen in Chatham in 1849. The date and place causes my imagination to fire up: that's the exact year and location at which the Presbyterian minister and missionary, Reverend William King, established Buxton, a community where freedmen and escaped slaves could settle. What if the first cardinals migrated north along with these underground railroad refugees, who built the farms, factories and schools of North and South Buxton? I picture incoming cardinals hovering over the incoming travellers like scarlet-winged blessings. The red birds were under less immediate pressure to establish themselves than the persecuted

Black refugees of Chatham were. While the Buxton community became a going concern with two thousand inhabitants by the 1860s, Curry notes it was 1901 before a first pair of breeding cardinals reached Point Pelee, the finger of land that stretches toward the American shore in Lake Erie and is therefore a major cross-the-lake migration route for birds and monarch butterflies. By 1914, Curry says, cardinals were fairly common around London, Ontario, but they were still rare in Hamilton when Owen Merriman made his first sighting on July 7, 1923. Ruby Mills, one of the founding members of the Bird Protection Society along with Merriman, also saw one that year, writing, "Its appearance here is most unusual."

Popular impressions around migration history are strange. Today, many people remain as unaware of the African village that existed on the mountain brow in Hamilton in the mid-nineteenth century as they are of Buxton, while just as many assume cardinals are indigenous to this region.

Curry says cardinals pushed northward into Ontario between 1900 and 1940 and, this time, he does offer some reasons. Essentially, urban sprawl and global warming have been good for cardinals. They moved north because of what Curry calls "climate warming" and the resulting shallower snow, as well as deforestation, the creation of edge habitats and easy meals at bird feeders. English sparrows and cardinals are here because of fossil fuels and urbanization: they like people, and people – except for the oyster-supper hunters in Streetsville – like them. Cities make warmer climates. Houses block wind and leak heat in winter. The flowers and trees in city gardens go to seed, giving seed eaters plenty to eat in winter, even if there isn't a bird feeder in every

yard. These urban yards offer tree cover, open lawns for foraging
and short flights, plus dense hedges for nesting and quick escape
from hawks. Not that hawks aren't happy about these arrangements: the number of sharp-shinned hawks in North America
has also increased with urbanization. There are more songbirds
in city yards for them to feed on.

A feeder in the yard produces effects that ripple out to Mexico
and Hudson Bay.

But if city living is good for sparrows and cardinals, why isn't
it good for breeding juncos? I can only guess. Perhaps, they were
pushed out by the bigger and more aggressive English sparrows
and red birds. Or, maybe it's the opposite – maybe juncos are
tougher than English sparrows and cardinals, and can survive in
harsher places like the Arctic, where these others can't survive.
Whatever the reason, it's become part of nature's cycle: juncos in
winter, sparrows and cardinals year-round.

Often, we think cities are outside of nature. Nature exists in
parks elsewhere – Banff or Algonquin or Yellowstone. Cities dis-
count nature. But if you look at what Curry calls the ubiquity of
the cardinal, you realize that everything we do in cities, let alone
out in the wilderness, has an effect.

We are *in it*. In Nature.

We sometimes think that because we've got heated bedrooms
and indoor plumbing that we have escaped nature, found ways to
live outside its laws. But taking down a cherry tree upsets the lives
of flowers and squirrels, and the shifted balance of juncos and cardinals reminds us the built city is still smack in the middle of nature.

Even the cycle of hunter and hunted continues right here
in this yard, from neighbourhood cats keeping an eye out for

chipmunks to red-tailed hawks screech-whistling overhead as they buzz oaks and maples, trying to scare up birds or squirrels. Consider the rough-legged hawks, the screech owls, or the time I was amazed to see a peregrine falcon land in our neighbour's Bing cherry tree.

Some of that cycle is even closer to home, though, than predators and their prey. A few winters back, I was sitting in the sunroom reading, when I heard a thump on the big picture window behind me. It was a sickening sound. I don't hear it as often now that the addition has been up for almost ten years, but back when it was new, we'd have one or two birds a year fly hard into one of the windows. I don't know why it happens – perhaps they see daylight through the windows on the other side and think there's an open path. Or maybe the reflection makes it look like a throughway. As with taking down the chokecherry, all that beautiful glass has thrown off the traffic routes.

I knew what the thump meant, so I got up to see if whoever had smashed into the glass was going to be all right. Down on the patio stones by the foundation of the house was a female cardinal, upright on her feet but obviously stunned. It's hard to tell what will happen at this point. Sometimes, the stunned bird will shake it off after a while and fly into the cedar hedge to recover. Other times, I've had to go out there with a broom and a dustpan.

Neither of these occurred. Instead, a sporty red male and brown female cardinal zoomed down to the mossy stones beside the downed bird. *Isn't that sweet,* I thought. *Friends have come to help.*

Not so. The male began pecking viciously at the stunned female with its thick seed-cracking beak, while the new female set up

Daniel Coleman

a shrill chirping that echoed off the basement wall. Appalled, I knocked on the window, trying to distract the aggressors, but the two kept at it without paying me the least notice. I began to wonder if those two had been chasing the injured bird. Maybe it was new in the neighbourhood and had trespassed on their territory. Perhaps that's why it misjudged the window.

Young cardinals look pretty much like females, so another troubling possibility is that these were parents chasing their young off to find its own place. I've heard of that happening. I'd be surprised, though, if they had a baby to chase off this far into winter.

I usually think it best to not interfere with nature. I never know when I'm interrupting something necessary. But after watching for another minute as the red male stabbed the stunned brown bird around its head, neck and eyes, I couldn't take it anymore. I shoved my feet into shoes and crunched down the icy steps, clapping my hands and shouting like a playground teacher. The attackers flicked up into the bare sweet cherry branches above.

It was cold out, and I hadn't stopped to put on a jacket – plus, I had somebody's chapter to read by this afternoon – so I went back in after one more glance at the bird on the stones, still catching its breath. About an hour later, I got up to put on tea and looked out to see what had happened. The brown bird was still there on the stones, her chest pumping in and out, blinking one black eye. I looked at the thermometer: minus ten. I wondered how long she could sit still and keep warm, how wounded she was. Sometimes a bird can break a wing smashing into a window – or its neck. I wondered how long she could sit there before one of our neighbourhood cats found her. So I put my shoes back on and crunched down the stairs again, loud, so she would know I was coming and wouldn't be startled. When I got within a few feet of her, she surprised me by darting into the cedar hedge.

So you *can* fly.

I see things like this – birds beating up on one another, taking advantage of one who's weak or wounded – and I realize that we have no clue at all. "Consider birds of the air ... Consider the lilies of the field," says the Bible. And I do. I try to consider them. But what exactly should a person consider? Jesus holds up the birds and lilies as beings who don't care about material trappings – fine clothes, a big house in the suburbs, a Lamborghini in the driveway. He says, "They neither sow nor reap . . . They do not toil." But considering them this way uses the lily and the bird as metaphors to make a human point. And it considers only the surface of their lives. If you have ever watched a harried set of cardinal parents trying to keep food in their chirping child's beak, you'll know that they're certainly toiling. And this isn't even touching on cardinal violence – the territorial fights, the pecking orders of the alpha male down to the youngest, weakest female.

Nature is sometimes hard to consider. It is too big and complex – and ceaselessly changing – to fit in our headspace, even though we have a long history of trying to make it do so. Even my anger at the bullies, my rushing out to defend the wounded – these are human judgments in which I impose my ideas of justice, of right and wrong, on the world beyond my ken. For all I know, I may have created a horror in the world of cardinals, right here in my yard. Maybe that stunned bird had just murdered its sibling, or crashed the parents' nest. Maybe it later grew up to be the tyrant of our neighbourhood. I don't know. I just glimpsed a little slice of their intersecting lives. Nature goes on, day in day out, whether we're watching and alert or not. Then for a minute or two, it grips our attention. We intervene. Break up the ruckus; maybe break rules whose logic we haven't learned. Fill an inlet, cut down a chokecherry, hang up a hummingbird feeder. Then we head back indoors and insert our feet in our slippers with little idea of what happened before or after.

CONSIDER, TOO, THE TRAFFIC of plants: compared to cardinals or squirrels, they seem to need less intervention, less traffic control. If there's movement in this yard, we assume it's going to depend on wings or legs. The rest, we think, stays put. That's what *planted* means, what *rooted* means. Flora fits our orderly mental maps better than fauna. It stays where we put it. It seems more manageable, more predictable.

I am therefore startled each spring when the white campion or the beardtongue perennials come up six or eight inches to the right or left of the ring I had set up around the plant the year before to keep its long stems from bending to the ground when the flowers fill with rain. It's as if those roots have little feet that skitter like crabs a few inches to the right or left at the start of each season. And so far I'm just talking about plants that stay in their root balls. I'm not talking yet about the ones with runners. They're called runners for good reason. Take ferns for example. I plant one this year and it sits where I put it. But unknown to me, it's sending out rhizomes under the surface, and next spring, there's a family of ferns spreading out over ten feet of ground. Two years later, they've made a thirty-foot suburb. Soon I'm digging out ferns and slicing through runners with a shovel.

And there's the mobility of seeds. Every year, it's a guessing game where the lamb's ears will come up. They thrive for a year or two in one spot, coming up thick and strong, three-foot-tall blue-grey shoots topped with long, skinny corncobs of tiny pink flowers. Their pollen-rich tips attract crowds of bees and bee flies. With oval leaves soft and thick as polar fleece, the flock of plants looks like it's clamped down onto its patch of garden forever. Its silver growth is so impressive that I don't notice the little leaves coming up on the opposite side of the yard, under the peonies or the coneflowers. Then, later in the year, the big colony starts to look withered and tired, as if some unseen force is drinking away its vitality. Before I know it, I'm digging out its last straggling and twisted stems, while across the yard, where I never bothered to look, a new colony is taking hold. In the years we've gardened here, we've had lamb's ears migrate across the yard four or five times – like sheep, always looking for new pasture. I imagine this migration can be credited to the mobility of seeds. Whether they blow around, get eaten by birds and dropped out who knows where in their guano, or are transported in the knapsacks of bees or ants, I don't know. But move they do, their motion as mysterious as underground water.

Even with runners and airborne or gut-borne seeds, I'm still describing local, minor plant traffic, not the dramatic movement going on among this garden's – pretty much any garden's – plants. Ninety percent of what we have planted here are immigrants: Korean boxwoods, Japanese maples, *Arum Italicum*, European wild ginger, Alberta spruce. Together, the plants in our garden constitute a global plant community. When we were planting this garden, we looked for height, size of spread and leaf shape. We settled on a colour palette and only planted flowers that bloom white, pink or purple. When we were putting this garden together, we considered look and appeal. We did not think about travellers and locals, foreigners and natives.

Recently, however, plant travel is drawing more and more notice. "Invasive plants are spreading through our natural eco-systems, urban landscapes and agricultural lands at an alarming rate," warns *Grow Me Instead: Beautiful Non-Invasive Plants for Your Garden*, a guide for gardeners put out by the Ontario Invasive Plant Council. The brochure lists worldwide human travel and trade as the first culprits in fomenting this colonial invasion. For this council, globalization is happening in our yard.

As happened when we imported English sparrows, it seems we settlers always meddle with the local mix. We are people on the move. But we don't just move ourselves; we take a lot of baggage with us. Our identity and self-worth is based on moving and improving: cutting down the trees and planting wheat, taking out the bunch berries and planting blueberries, ripping out the clover and putting in lawns. Out with the wild grape and in with the English ivy. We carry on an international traffic in plants. We crave the exotic, love plants from other parts of the world that bloom longer, produce more grain per acre, have tougher stems. So we tear out the local and plant the import. We graft and hybridize, patent a new cultivar, modify a gene.

In the world of gardening, one of many Ontarians' favourite areas to choose plants from is Japan. Looking around this yard alone, I have a Bloodgood Japanese maple, a Crimson Queen Japanese maple, a Japanese willow, lots of Japanese spurge and half a dozen Japanese painted ferns. I imagine we do this because Japanese garden aesthetics focus on leaf colour and texture, and not so much on the colour of flowers. You don't have to wait for blooms; the beauty is subtler and longer lasting.

Most of the plants in our garden are relatively innocent and not too aggressive or intrusive. Here on our little fenced property, we trim and clip before they get out of hand and run riot. But this yard is only the part we know, the segment we see every day. Consider those lamb's ears appearing wherever they will every year or two. We don't really know whose seeds are being eaten by birds and then spread into the fields and woodlands around us, maybe even kilometres away. And we don't know what happens once they're there.

It's possible to see what can happen though. Mrs. Forbes planted Japanese spurge and Eurasian periwinkle as ground covers under the white pines and maples down our back slope. She also planted native woodland species like red and white trilliums, trout lilies and three or four different kinds of ferns. Ever since, the ground covers have done the job of holding the soil in place on the slope, preventing erosion. But the spurge and the periwinkle have run right down the hill, under the fence and into the land below. There's a little pond of periwinkle behind our neighbour's place to the east, escapees from our slope, heading off to explore the Ancaster Creek valley below. The ostrich ferns she planted make a beautiful, waist-high canopy of lime green all the way down our slope, and they have sent runners throughout the surrounding woods. Who knows how far they will eventually travel?

All this is nature at work. Whether local or imported, all plants spread. And as for imports, no place on earth is a sealed island. Exchange happens. Even if humans don't bring English sparrows to North America, climate change eventually brings cardinals.

However, humans are active participants. Because we like the look of them or because they'll feed us, we bring non-native plants to North America. But a deer does the same thing when burrs catch on its fur as it moves from one valley to the next, and bird intestines carry seeds from god-knows-where as they migrate from here to Nicaragua. So why do people get worked up about invasive plants, as if they are immigrants to be stopped at the border?

The *Grow Me Instead* brochure admits that most imports aren't too much of a problem. It focuses more on the aggressive, invasive ones that reduce biodiversity by wiping out the territory of other plants. This reduction not only narrows the number of food supplies for animals, insects and birds, but it also makes a weaker ecosystem, devoid of the strength and resiliency of a thriving ecosystem.

Nonetheless, it's still not easy to make a firm judgment between locals and imports. Indigenous plants have had time to evolve here. Over centuries, they've gotten used to the amount of rain and sun and winter we get. They've developed ways of surviving, of adapting to the cycle of the seasons here. They've been at it for ages – all the way back to the strawberry roots and the three sisters that Atsi'tsiaká:ion imported from the hole in the sky. But how long do imports stay foreign? Beans and corn and squash have been cultivated here for thousands of years now, while the Shasta daisies we grow in this garden have been around here for only a hundred years. Still, the daisies seem pretty well adapted to this place. The hotter and drier Hamilton gets, the better they seem to do. So at what point do we admit that they've adapted? Made the crossing and settled in?

When does an immigrant become a local?

One measure could have to do with how the import deals with the long-time locals. Take a newcomer like English ivy. It grows vigorously, covering the walls of buildings with its dark green mat. Its shiny leaves feature distinctive, prominent veins etched in white. Its young leaves have five lobes – somewhat like a maple leaf – but they lose the lobes and become heart shaped as they grow older. Ivy is so tenacious that you almost cannot kill it. I know because I have tried. There's a stem of ivy that had been planted on the east side of our house back in Mrs. Forbes's day. More than ten years ago, we dug it out, ran the stone side-walk past where it had been and planted clematis instead. Every year, that ivy stem sends out new leaves and shoots. I'll find them grabbing onto the clematis and trying to strangle it. So I pull them off and rip the stem out by what I think are the roots. Next year, same thing. Without applying chemicals, I have not been able to eradicate it.

But that's what ivy does. It overwhelms anything that occupies any space to which it aspires. It respects no one, gives no one else a break. It considers no space sacred, no land holy. It will colonize anything, including the brick and masonry of the house or the bark of a white pine. It makes no difference if the ground is loamy and rich, drained or soggy, clay or sand. Full shade, full sun – no difference. If there were a plant with ambitions of establishing an empire, it would be English ivy. It grows from

Ireland and Scandinavia to Turkey and Sicily. Now it's all over North America. That's why the Ontario Invasive Plant Council has English ivy on its Most-Detested, Dead-or-Alive list.

Like English sparrows, ivy was introduced in the nineteenth century. These immigrant plants fight it out with the locals right here in our yard, alongside the ongoing struggles between cardinals and juncos. They have unlooked-for effects, just like our cutting down of the chokecherry did. They transform themselves and the neighbourhood, like hummingbirds or dog-day cicadas do. These newcomers reach down into the mystery of earth, tangle roots with local populations, compete for nutrients, light and water. They become part of the local scene, sometimes as allies, sometimes as aggressors. Whatever we think of them, they're here now, part of our own being here.

Anyone attending to the birds of this air and the lilies of this garden will see that there's no hibernating in this backyard, no hiding one's head in the sand. Even the creatures who live in that sand, like cicadas, travel from a domain we can't see and don't know too much about to another one high overhead. We hear their songs shimmering in the air, but they're still usually invisible to us. To read the biography of this one small place in the city is to read of intercontinental connections, transnational travel. Considering the birds of this air and the flowers of this garden puts me in direct touch with environmental farm politics in Costa Rica and melting arctic ice flows in Hudson Bay. It makes me wonder about import and export, immigration and indigenization. This place is no place to hide. It is no island.

Many times, I've come out into this yard to enjoy the quiet, the stillness. And it *is* quiet; it is still – compared to human-made noises like planes on a runway or trucks on an overpass. But it doesn't take thirty seconds in this yard to see that this quiet place is busy, alive with movement, humming with activity. The point is that nature itself – Creation – *is* this quiet traffic. It is constantly creating, constantly moving, constantly communicating, constantly exchanging and trading. Every day this yard demonstrates that even the smallest, humblest, most inconsequential, sleepy place in the world sparks and echoes the global flow, its electric hum, its ceaseless, ongoing life.

Yardwork

YARDWORK COULD BE CONSIDERED lawn care – the work of landscape maintenance or, at a grand estate, grounds keeping. These terms convey the image of people intimate with their parcel of land, who express their care for it by clipping and mowing, edging and staking. A garden domesticated and manicured, not free or wild: creation controlled. With this set of images in mind, an ecologist might have some disdain for yardwork, at the way humans meddle with nature.

But this is the reality of life in the twenty-first century. For better or worse, we and our cities are in nature, and nature is absolutely shaped by our being in it. Rick Potts, director of the Human Origins Program at the National Museum of Natural History in Washington, DC, follows a growing number of geologists who call the epoch of *Homo sapiens* the Anthropocene, which follows the Holocene and Pleistocene periods and refers to the period during which upright two-legged mammals spread around the world and reshaped it. He says, for instance, that today humans use, destroy or occupy eighty-three percent of the world's viable land surface and that most of the world's energies have been bent to serve human needs.

Whether for good or ill, humans are clipping and chopping at creation all over the planet, and the chances of nature being free to go its own way are pretty much nil. There's no point in trying to rewind to a prehuman time, to some fantastical pre-Anthropocene purity. Hano'gyeh the muskrat dug up earth from the bottom of the sea so that Atsi'tsiaká:ion could plant her strawberries and other plants for food and medicine. According to the Six Nations story of origin, the Anthropocene began with digging and planting to help each other survive. I'm sure the animal and bird people didn't mind having strawberries, corn, beans and squash to supplement the watery diet they had before that first woman fell into their world. The point, then, is to make sure that our digging and clipping is about care and sharing, keeping the seven generations in mind, rather than pillaging and hoarding, which makes for collective suicide.

Compared to the long reach of time signalled by Sky Woman and the Anthropocene, a biography of one backyard in one post-industrial city is small potatoes. But the daily work of care and sharing and maintenance is never very visible within massive concepts of time and space. Caring is intimate. It's hard to care about abstractions, about something I haven't seen myself, something far away and long ago or light years into the future. It's a lot easier to care about one life that I know closely than about millions and billions of lives I've only heard about. Once I know that one life intimately, I have a better chance of caring about others like it.

That is why I've been trying to share the layered biography of this one backyard. *Bios* + *graphia* = life + writing: putting words to life, or giving life to words. Of course, one of the first questions about any biography is why this particular life matters. Some biographies are about celebrities, famous people whose prominence makes the choice obvious. A biography of Janis Joplin or Joseph Stalin or Nelson Mandela matters in the same way a coffee-table book on Yellowstone, the Dead Sea or Banff National

Park matters. We've all heard of them, so the question of who cares never comes up. But why write a biography about someone few people have ever heard of? Why write a biography for one pretty average backyard in a pleasant but everyday neighbourhood, in a naturally blessed but abused city landscape?

I've already tried to show how any humble place, even in the Anthropocene – especially in the Anthropocene – is actually a hub of global connections. So a biography of this tiny, insignificant place is not inward-looking parochialism. This insignificant backyard books regular flights to the Arctic Circle and to Costa Rica. Telling the life of this one place is a way of digging out from our impressions that it's merely one static place, stuck in its little urban lot, going nowhere. Telling its stories is a way of reanimating the way we imagine place – this place, any place. What needs reanimating isn't nature, isn't the life going on in this yard, with the mandibles eating our grassroots, the beaks finding nourishment in the cracks and fissures we don't even know are there. What needs reanimating is our ability to see, to perceive what's already going on, to hear what's already being said. And to do that, we need to change who we think we are, who we think is doing the hearing and looking.

In the first poem of a cycle of poems entitled "Moral Proverbs and Folk Songs," the Spanish poet Antonio Machado put it this way:

The eye you see is not
an eye because you see it;
it is an eye because it sees you.

This yard has eyes in it. They see me. They see me, they see my neighbours, and they wonder and think. They evaluate us, deciding how much harm we could do, how peaceful we are, whether we're edgy or content, distracted or calm. They try to tell us things. They hold our human gaze and bow their heads down, then up. Down, then up.

I don't know what much of this already existing communication means. Most of us don't. Most people in this city are descended from the people who move. We haven't lived in the neighbourhood long enough to know what these eyes and bowings are saying. Vine Deloria Jr., a Standing Rock Sioux from the Oglala Lakota territory in South Dakota, once explained that settlers haven't been on this continent very long, nor do our families tend to settle in one place for significant periods of time, so we don't have much chance to develop a deep relationship with the environment. I've lived here a little less than twenty years, and in that time I've tried to learn how to listen to this place, but that's a drop in the bucket compared to people in the area whose families go back several thousand years. Even the Binkleys only arrived a little over two hundred years ago. No wonder we don't understand what other forms of life are trying to say.

Which is why, in trying to hear the stories this place might have to tell, I've tried to pay particular attention, among all the various accounts and tales, to the longhouse people's stories. They have had a chance to listen and learn in the Great Lakes and Carolinian forest country for generations upon generations. And that long, multigenerational observation has taught them some advanced things, like the antibiotic and calming effects of white pine aerosols that make it a tree of peace. Sadly, much of what Hodinöhsö:ni' people know has been suppressed and discarded by those of us who arrived later on and who were oblivious to the eyes that see us. In the certitude of that blinkered condition, our ancestors built residential schools like the Mohawk Institute in Brantford, near the Six Nations reserve. They did their best to destroy the memories carried in the Hodinöhsö:ni' languages, and to replace those memories with new housing starts and television. Nonetheless, enough longhouse people have kept track of the old words and the stories they carry; enough have shared these things with our generation – indeed, in our own languages and technologies, including TV – that it's still possible to learn from the stories that remain.

Even newcomers like me can pick up the sense of how important and fragile these place-stories are. Because it's only by words and stories that we can keep track of what has gone on in a place. Maybe this is what is meant when the Bible says that in the beginning was the Word. Maybe it's saying that words and expressiveness pre-existed us and our arrival. And that it's only through tuning into these local words that we collectively can figure out what our place – this place – has been saying all this time, what it's still saying. Words and stories and talk are how we learn from what those who lived here before us understood about the place. They keep us alive in this place, and keep this place alive in us.

Creation is expressive. Expressiveness is Creation.

This expressive liveliness is mobile. This is the salient thing about bios + graphia: it keeps being told, being recorded. It doesn't stop. It takes what is apparently fixed – the self, a life – and tracks its movement, and by doing so reminds us of the mobility in what seems to be its solid and immutable objects.

Life stories reanimate this movement, this energy and liveliness, with the flimsiest of elements: the word. What can sharing the life stories of this one backyard hope to achieve? We all know that ultimately, words themselves are weak, even when we assemble the best ones possible. They lean on one another to make sense. We know what one means by its size and shape compared to the next one. Strangely, that rickety quality is what makes words perfect. As Jacques Ellul pointed out in *The Humiliation of the Word*, their flimsiness comes from their mobility. They only mean by moving, by comparing one and then the next and the next. Big, tall, long, wide, deep – they all point at largeness, but they each name a different kind of largeness by comparison with each other. The word "broken" in broken pine reminds us that we know which pine we mean only by family resemblance and then by the differences in the family. Or – like a house of cards with its diamonds, hearts, spades and clubs – by suit, and then by rank and number within the suit.

Following someone's words is also movement. Whether you're listening to someone over coffee or reading a sentence in the paper, you have to stay in the flow to know what the sentence means. You have to wait until the end of the statement, the end of the chapter, to know what it adds up to. Ellul said that this having to wait for the unfolding of the sentence or the story is different from taking a photograph. You look at a camera-made image and you get the impression that you're seeing the whole thing, the entire event, all the evidence you need, in one moment. It makes you feel like you already know the story. That's why photography and video are so convincing in a courtroom. If you can get a picture of someone pulling the trigger or dumping coal tar in the harbour, you've got the evidence you need.

Compared to pictures, words are time-consuming and uncertain. It takes days and weeks to transcribe the witnesses' testimonies, then to read the reams and reams of conflicting evidence. Words take time because they are easy to mistake, to mishear and misread. Despite their weak and wobbly character, words are also absolutely, if hopelessly, perfect for trying to track and record the life of a place, or for that matter any life, any *bios*. The delay and imprecision of words, their vulnerability to missing the mark and making mistakes – these qualities of words reduce our ability to take listeners, and the beings we're talking about, prisoner. "Place persistently eludes our grasp, so long as grasp is what it is," writes poet and ecologist Don McKay. Finding the right words for the inappellable, the unnameable, "doesn't mean solving the mystery," he adds, "it means setting it to music" – which does not pin it down but puts it in motion and gives it wings. The lives we tell stories about, the ongoingness and mobility of living things, always escapes our control, like the creek John and I watched in delight pouring over the escarpment, completely evading the huge concrete channel that had been built to contain it.

Telling stories about a place, making multi-layered words about this backyard in this city, is an effort of care, a way to pay attention to its unfolding life, to free it from our tendency to package it as a piece of real estate, an immobile object, a stereotype. The Hammer. The Lunch Bucket. Steel Town. Rust Belt City. Armpit of Ontario. Even the various efforts to rebrand this Dish With One Spoon as the City of Waterfalls, the Ambitious City, or the Best Place to Raise a Child – they all tend to put the place in concrete shoes, cram it in a garbage bin, put a price tag on it, or stuff it in a promotional package.

BUT LAND ITSELF IS humble, too, like words and water. It's got their same fragility and ongoingness. It doesn't usually push itself to the front, doesn't tend to grab the megaphone. So a person generally has to put in some effort, some work, to pay it proper notice. And noticing usually requires some retuning on our part.

So often, we've got earbuds plugged into our heads, or we're staring at our smart phones as we walk down the sidewalk. The only time we look up and actually pay the place any mind is when we're visiting properties with a realtor. Or when the land rebels about something: regurgitates the DDT we've been spraying on it, coughs up sour gases when we've been fracking it, shakes its bones in an earthquake for reasons unknown to us. Otherwise, land just keeps living its life, at the edges of our notice, day in day out.

I once heard Ima Johnson, a Six Nations clan mother and elder-in-residence at McMaster, say that if you want people to be comfortable with you, if you want them to enjoy your company and wish to visit you again, you've got to notice them. Say, "Good to see you. I'm glad you came. How are you doing?" You know, show some courtesy and interest. If you don't pay the person any mind, don't greet them or make them feel noticed and welcome, they're not going to want to come around next time, are they?

It's the same thing with all our non-human neighbours, too, she said. If we don't say hello to the clean water, don't say thanks for being so refreshing and nice to drink, maybe clean water won't want to visit us anymore. If we don't notice that earthworms are enriching our soil, that pine needles are calming our lungs, that raccoons are cleaning up our garbage, then maybe they'll get tired of being taken for granted. The chickadees and the coneflowers might say, there's no point in being friendly with these people. All they do is take. They never notice us at all.

I hear an echo of Ima's words when the American poet Gary Snyder says, "An ethical life is one that is mindful, mannerly, and has style. . . . The world is not only watching, it is listening too. A rude or thoughtless comment about a Ground Squirrel or a Flicker or a Porcupine will not go unnoticed."

So words may be fragile and uncertain, but they are still important. It's just plain rude to talk about a place as if it's only value is financial, as an object whose resources we can just take. To talk out loud about how much we could get for the Tree of Peace, Ancaster Creek, the ruby-throated hummingbird, or the Easter-morning antler. Imagine if people in your neighbourhood talked about you that way, as if your only value is in how much you make. As if you were an object, like they do in a slave market or a boardroom.

We've had centuries of this kind of rudeness. So much that it's become normal. We talk about land as property. Back in the early days of our modern legal system, the philosopher John Locke explained that what made Europeans different from uncivilized people was that we had private property, and we had established clear laws about how to buy and sell it. The problem with Native North Americans – he called them "savages" – was that they didn't have our idea of property, and so they had no way to develop a civilized constitution.

It's clear that he had never heard of the kayaneren'tsherakowa. Or, if he had heard of it, he couldn't see it as a civilized constitution, because it didn't start with dividing up property. Rather than starting with dividing up things, it started with connecting them, for making peace, friendship and respect – not just between humans and humans, but between everybody who shared a place. We tend to think of treaties the way John Locke thought about law, as mechanisms for trading property. But the Hodinöhsö:ni' law of peace is based on the idea of treaties between people and all residents in an ecosystem. That's why longhouse people have a clan, for example, to name some folks in their community for their special relationships and responsibilities with the deer or bears or turtles in their neighbourhood.

The understanding of the living, breathing land, with all its inhabitants – who themselves are living, breathing and talking – as neighbours with whom you have treaties has been dismissed by Euro-American societies as rude in that old, disparaging sense. They did not simply mean a lack of manners but being primitive and brutish. Rude, as in crude and unfinished: lacking skill, precision, education or knowledge – a state of ignorance. Native people's politeness, their ways of noticing and saying thanks to the animals, plants and minerals for maintaining clean air and fresh water were not just disparaged, but actually outlawed as practices both pagan and savage.

But you have to wonder about these designations when you look at the bill we all have to pay to clean up Randle Reef or to treat lung cancer in this city. The costs of toxins in the watershed, the price to pay for disappeared species – it's clearly time to rethink what's rude and primitive, what's style and good manners.

In writing this biography for this small place in the city, I'm aiming at different measurements for style and politeness, for what we think of as civilization. If we can at least start to notice the place itself, its wonder and beauty, even if it's precisely in the middle of one of the most put upon places in North America, perhaps we can turn around our thinking so that instead of dumping ground or real estate, it becomes the place where first woman touched down, limestone cliffs rose up and deer reminded us to use a good mind. Perhaps we come to think of where we live as a dish with one spoon.

"If to record is to love the world," writes the poet Roo Borson, "let this be an entry." Likewise, may my effort to record, in the flimsiness of words, what's going on in this one small yard in this one neighbourhood in one average city be one such entry. I'm no expert, and I know I've missed more wonders than I've named, but I'm tired of my own history of constantly moving away from the place where I live, literally and in my mind. I'm tired of economies, politics and laws that are based on rejecting the place, treating it with disrespect, with disregard. Tired of a culture of cut and move on, of the arrogance and casual bad manners that treat the world of everyday wonders like it's not listening, not watching, not alive, not got feelings or hopes.

My instincts are saying that, in the end, the answer to Randle Reef or carbon monoxide in the air we breathe is, finally, love. And the first step to caring about the place is as simple as being willing to pay attention – to start noticing. You don't have to move to some wilderness or even Algonquin Park to see the incredible resiliency and optimism of the many lives around us. It's all around, going on in the crawling universe under our lawns and sidewalks, in the trickle of water from roof to downspout to soil and gravel bed below, in the pneumatic wonder of trees, even broken ones. Whether we're watching or not, it's going on right here in the city.

This past May, Wendy and I spent a whole Saturday working in the garden, trimming hedges, chopping up and bundling
broken branches, digging and spreading compost, weeding and
transplanting. Doing our yardwork. When we took a breather,
Wendy arched her back to stretch out a kink, and, head tilted to
the blue sky, said, "Being out here restores my soul." After we'd
worked through the morning and into the early afternoon, we
placed the cushions on the furniture in the little back patio and
put our feet up on the footstools. We fell asleep, the two of us, for
twenty minutes in the sun, the pines talking quietly overhead in
the breathing air. Eventually Wendy stretched, raised a hand to
shade her eyes from the sun, turned to me and said, again, "Being
out here feels good."

I asked, "Why? What's good about it?"

"I don't know. It grounds me, fills my heart. The beauty."

Right behind her, the blaze of white down the middle of a
hosta leaf winked at me as a breeze turned it slightly. *Undulata
variegata.* You don't have to know Latin for your eyes to smile
at these wavy green and white leaves. Each leaf on the six-foot-
round plant has a blaze in the middle and long rib lines running from stem to tip that bow out wide in the middle and
rush together to the point. Yet each leaf is completely distinct,
every single one different from the next in size, shape and colour. The blaze of white is sometimes a smooth, broad band,
sometimes a series of flames, sometimes jags and spurts down
the tongue of the leaf. Right behind the hosta, I could see the
white bleeding heart, with ranks of fifteen or twenty flowers on
each branch hanging like a series of heart-shaped bells, their
clappers dangling silent from the tip of each one. They are crisp

and white as dress shirts, swinging softly above their deep-cut, green leaves.

Everywhere you turn your eye, it is like this. Each being is distinct, utterly itself, never duplicated – a whole world of its own. Your eye can stop on leaf or petal or wing or berry and never run out of wonder. Tiny weeds spring from the gaps between the flagstones by my footstool. They are only three inches high. Their stems are slender green hairs, and on the ends of each a spray of pristine white flowers. They're so small my eye can't really count the petals, let alone detect stamens or anthers. I step into the house for the magnifying glass. Even with my nose two inches from the pungent moss and my eye peering through the lens, it doesn't really tell me who they are. Or, at least, what I see through the glass doesn't match up to any of the flowers in my *Field Guide to North American Wildflowers*. The closest thing is perhaps some kind of chickweed. These flowers are an eighth of an inch across. Through the magnifying glass, my finger holding their stem is a huge pink zeppelin beside their tiny filigree. They've got such deep divisions in each of their five petals I think there are ten of them. The magnification lets me see the architecture better. The *Field Guide's* section on the parts of a flower tells me the orange-brown knots on the ends of these skinny filaments are the pollen-bearing anthers. They thrust out like this so bees and other insects can brush off the pollen. A bee beside this flower would be a lumbering behemoth. Down lower are the stigma pads, where the flower collects pollen, though hopefully not its own. Most flowers reject inbreeding by spitting out their own pollen if it gets stuck on the stigmas. Down below, where the filaments holding up the anthers and stigmas join, there's a bulge, which is where the flower keeps its eggs. It's waiting for the right kind of pollen to land, get watered and enriched in the stigma, and then begin the journey down the filament to the ovary and the egg.

Right here. In this crack between stones in the patio, is a weed you can hardly see without artificial help. It's all going on. This matrix of intelligence, transformation, selection, commerce with passing insects, sex and reproduction. It's as complex as the two-hundred-foot oak down the hill, as intimate as anybody's bedroom.

I'm still on hands and knees with my butt in the air when a clutch of black-capped chickadees lands in the Bloodgood Japanese maple. They talk quietly in tiny, high-voiced peeps – sharp, but not urgent like cardinals or jays. They sound as if they are muttering to each other. They hop among the branches, heads cocking from side to side. They're searching for bugs crawling on the bark or hidden in crevices where stems and branches join. Haskell says that chickadees and other birds can see one more colour range than humans can. They perceive the three primaries that we do, but they also see ultraviolet. This fourth colour range makes insects jump out, like white shirts under black light. It gives me a strange pleasure to know that the superpowered eyes of one chickadee or another have inspected every millimetre of this yard, no stone or leaf unturned. There's a whole system of communication going on between them. Their tiny peeps are more for themselves than anyone else as they forage. After a few minutes, one of the bunch flips up to a branch and pipes out the two-note "Spring's here!" Who knows what it means in her language. Is this about territory? Our flock is here, stay away? Is it about sex? Or food? The glory of the day? Whatever it means, it's clearly communication of some kind. Perhaps she's talking to me, and I've never stayed around long enough to figure out what she's saying.

There are so many stories about talking animals and the people who understand them, from Doctor Dolittle to Saint Francis. Sometimes it gets made into miracles or mysticism. But if Vine Deloria Jr. is right, it's really a matter of people paying attention long enough to learn what's being said, like any other language. If I don't understand what she means when she bursts out with her signature chick-a-dee-dee-dee, it's not her fault. It's more that I've never developed the good manners Ima Johnson was talking about, never been taught my chickadee *p*'s and *q*'s. I've been encouraged to think what she has to say is nonsense, makes no sense.

But maybe, even at this late age – in my own life and that of our culture – maybe we can learn better behaviour. Learn something about the good mind – about saying hello and offering greetings. Maybe, if we can retune ourselves, if we decide it's worth paying attention not just to our own needs but to the whole neighbourhood of bursting, mind-boggling, ongoing life, a little yardwork could turn this place back into a Dish with One Spoon, a holy land right here, a place that's always good for the soul.

Acknowledgements

THIS BIOGRAPHY AIMS TO feature the lives that intersect in this one urban backyard, so it tends to downplay people in its effort to credit the birds, watershed, trees, sedimentary layers, animals, weather and insects that make up the life of this place. Accordingly, I acknowledge here, with gratitude and awe, the manifold, everyday and startling life that makes itself in this place season after season. Long may it be so.

My effort to record this yard's ongoing life necessarily places me, the first-person observer, as subject of many of the sentences in this book. This grammatical convention contributes to the illusion that writers make books alone, but of course we write not only in conversation with other writers' books, but also with friends and sympathizers and mentors who advise, comment, opine and discern along with us. I am grateful to friends and colleagues who heard or read portions of this book in various stages of its development. These include Phanuel Antwi, Timothy Bascom,

Nathan Coleman, Lawrence Hill, Paul Lisson, Geoff Martin, Rick Monture, Michelle Peek and Jenny Ward. Ven Begamudré, Gary Geddes, Anne Simpson and John Terpstra, each of whom were at different times the Mabel Pugh Taylor Writer-in-Residence at McMaster University, read the entire manuscript at various stages of its development and offered generous and incisive comments. John Terpstra put the manuscript through a necessary, fine-meshed sieve, and Matthew Zantingh, student of literature and the urban environment, offered from his rich storehouse of knowledge thoughtful comments on the entire manuscript. Jane Watt brought her inimitable wit and sensitivity to an intensive and crucial edit of a penultimate draft. Noelle Allen, publisher at Wolsak & Wynn, understood the spirit of the book from the start, and then engaged in a round of fierce and lively edits that challenged and enhanced my writing. Andrew Wilmot and Ashley Hisson gave the final manuscript a very careful edit, and I am grateful for their keen attention to every word and sentence. Book designers rarely get mentioned in acknowledgements because their work comes after the Acknowledgements page has been completed. Marijke Friesen brought together font size, spacing, title pages and cover design to create the pleasure to eyes and fingers that you hold in your hands. The team at Wolsak & Wynn has made every effort to make the publishing of this book a rewarding experience. Taylor Gibson, of Deyohahá:ge: Indigenous Knowledge Centre, speaks and writes several of the Six Nations languages. I am thankful to him for reading through the glossary to this book and checking with language experts at Gawęnawihse' Onõda'gega' (Onondaga Language Program) on the Six Nations Reserve to ensure my approximations of Hodinöhsö:ni' words and spellings are as accurate as possible. Michael Gallant made the beautiful charcoal drawings that grace this book. It was a huge pleasure to discuss the drawings with him as he developed the concepts that inform each one. I cannot express adequately my gratitude for these friends' care and commitment to making this book as strong and readable as possible.

THE ECOSYSTEM OF FRIENDSHIP that nourished this project is diverse and replete. I am fortunate to work with a stimulating, generous, critically alert and warmly supportive group of colleagues and friends at McMaster University that has included over the years Jane Aronson, Nadine Attewell, Nancy Bouchier, Sarah Brophy, Chandrima Chakraborty, Ken Cruikshank, Juliet Daniel, Amber Dean, Patrick Deane, Jeffery Donaldson, Bernice Downey, Jeanette Eby, Donald Goellnicht, Marvin Gunderman, Janice Hladki, Mary Koziol, Travis Kroeker, Rick Monture, Susie O'Brien, Gaby Moyal and Mary O'Connor, Grace Pollock, Mary Silcox, Peter Walmsley, Gary and Joy Warner, Vanessa Watts, Carol Wood, Lorraine York and Gena Zuroski. A second, overlapping, community of elders, teachers and learners at Deyohahá:ge: Indigenous Knowledge Centre at Six Nations Polytechnic have stimulated and enriched my thinking while I was working on this book. Some of them also work at McMaster. They include: Patrick Byrne, Kaitlin Debicki, Tom Deer, Jessie Forsyth, Bonnie Freeman, Taylor Gibson, Jeremy Haynes, Rick Hill, Susan Hill, Tanis Hill, Rebecca Jamieson, Ima Johnson, Lottie Keye, Carrie McMullin, Rick Monture, Sandra Muse, Stephanie Pile, Bertha and Hubert Skye and Trish Van Katwyk. I am also deeply grateful to the energetic and meticulous love for learning of Carol Binkley and Mary McBain, whose research in the Binkley family history not only helped me avoid major errors but also stimulated my energy for finishing this project.

I LEARNED TO LIFT my eyes to the birds, forests and hills by growing up in a family that understands these elements of creation to be an important language for living, so this book has its roots in the Coleman family's birdwatching, lake-loving, tent-holidaying, garden-growing lexicon. My love and thanks go to all of my globally dispersed family – my parents, Murray and Bea; siblings, Sharon, John and Marianne; and their spouses and growing families, which contain an inordinate number of birders whose eyes scan the skies in Chile, Ethiopia, Australia, British Columbia, Alberta, Saskatchewan and Manitoba. My appreciation for family and place has been enriched and extended by the Saskatchewan-based Berkan family, whose identification with their prairie home gave me my first sense of rootedness in Canada. My feeling of purpose and energy is sustained by a community of friends near and far, including Tim Bascom, Ven Begamudré, David Chariandy, Julie Gellner, Dave Gray, Timothy Long and Brenda Beckman-Long, Grant and Caleb Moore and Dana Antaya Moore, Barbara Mutch, Gary and Carla Nelson, Jim Peck, Linda Warley, Jane Watt, Cam and Joan Yates, Rod McDonald and Mary Jane Yates.

ALL THE YARDWORK THAT led to this book was done in the companionship of Wendy Coleman, who makes life beautiful, dynamic and purposeful every day.

Glossary

*Please see the note on pronouncing Hodinöhsö:ni' words at the end of this glossary.

Anishinaabe – (Anishinaabewin or Ojibway language) means "original good people," the name for themselves used by the Odawa, Ojibway, Potawatomi and other people of the Algonquin language family.

A'nó:wara – (Mohawk language, spelled Hanyadengona in Onondaga) turtle, in the Creation Story the great turtle received Sky Woman onto her back and grew into the continent now known as North America.

Anthropocene – (English) the epoch of *Homo sapiens* that follows the Holocene and Pleistocene geological periods, and refers to the era in which human activities have had a major impact on Earth's geology and ecosystems.

Atsi'tsiaká:ion – (Mohawk, known as Awe(n)h'i' in Onondaga) means Mature Blossoms, the Sky World woman in the

Hodinöhsö:ni' Creation Story who fell through the hole in the sky and onto the great turtle's back.

Attawandaron – (Iroquoian language) the Iroquoian-speaking people, referred to by early French explorers at *"la Nation neutre,"* who lived at the Head-of-the-Lake and tried to maintain diplomatic relations with both the Hodinöhsö:ni' Confederacy to the southeast and the Huronian Alliance to the north.

De'hae'yawa:kho' – (Onondaga, spelled Tharonhywá:kon in Mohawk) means Skyholder, the good-minded twin brother in the Creation Story; he was later known as Shonkwaya'tíson (Mohawk), the Creator.

Dish with One Spoon – (English) see Sewatokwa'tshera't

Great Law of Peace – (English) see Kayaneren'tsherakowa

Hano'gyeh – (Onondaga, spelled Anò:kien in Mohawk) muskrat

Hodä:he' – (Onondaga) Guardian of the Standing Tree, Sky World being in Hodinöhsö:ni' Creation Story; his wife fell through the hole in the sky and onto the great turtle's back.

Hodinöhsö:ni' – (Seneca spelling, more often spelled "Haudenosaunee" in French and English texts) People who build the house, those who are building the longhouse; refers to the Iroquoian Confederacy of originally Five Nations – Mohawk, Oneida, Onondaga, Cayuga and Seneca – until the Tuscarora joined the Confederacy in the early eighteenth century, making them Six Nations. Others, such as small groups of Delaware, Tutelo and Nanticoke people, also adhere to the longhouse confederacy.

Ha-yĕnt-watha – (Mohawk, sometimes spelled Hyenwatha, and corrupted in Henry Wadsworth Longfellow's made-up myth as Hiawatha) The first man to accept Peacemaker's message of the Law of Peace and the inventor of wampum as an antidote for his grief.

Head-of-the-Lake – (English) term referring to the area at the western end of Lake Ontario that came into common usage between 1788 and 1793, when the townships around Hamilton Harbour and Cootes Paradise were surveyed and named. Likely derived from Indigenous references to the end of navigation at this end of Lake Ontario and the need to portage up the escarpment to proceed further west or south.

Iroquois – (English, likely a French corruption from the Algonquian word, *Irinakhoiw*) means "real snakes" or "adder people," a slur referring to members of the Hodinöhsö:ni' Confederacy.

Iroquoian languages – (English) the family of eastern North American languages extending from Cherokee and Susquehannock to Huron-Petun and the languages of the Six Nations.

Kaniatarí:io – (Mohawk) nice or beautiful lake, likely origin for the name "Ontario."

Kanien'kehá:ka – (Mohawk language) "people of the flinty ground," known today as Mohawks.

Kayaneren'tsherakowa – (Mohawk) "the great niceness," "the great warmth," and, most commonly, "the great law of peace." Commonly referred to as the Constitution of the Hodinöhsö:ni' Confederacy established by the Peacemaker, it is as much a spiritual as it is a legislative code.

Leucism – (English) a condition in which there is partial loss of pigmentation in an animal, resulting in white, pale or patchy colouration of the skin, hair, feathers, scales or cuticle, but not the eyes. Unlike albinism, it is caused by a reduction in multiple types of pigment, not just melanin.

Michi Saagiig – (Anishinaabemowin language) subgroup of Anishinaabe peoples who settled around the Head-of-the-Lake region and especially at the mouth of the Credit River after the Huron and Attawandaron were removed from this region by the Hodinöhsö:ni' in the mid-seventeenth century. "Mississauga" is an English approximation of this name.

Mohawk – (English) refers to Kanien'kehá:ka people from the Mohawk River region in northeastern New York. I know of two stories about the origins of the term "Mohawk": one, from Brian Maracle's *Back on the Rez*, suggests it was derived from an Algonquian insult meaning "cannibal"; the second asserts that when the Dutch arrived in Kanien'kehá:ka territory in the early seventeenth century, they heard the Algonquian Mohicans refer to the Kanien'kehá:ka as *Maw Unk Lin* (Bear Place People), which they transliterated as "Mohawk."

Ohnehta'kowa – (Mohawk) the tree of the long leaves or needles (Eastern White Pine, in English), which the Peacemaker designated as *Onerahtase'ko:wa*, the Tree of Peace, whose white roots people could follow from the four directions of the world to find the way of peace. The White Pine's needles grow in clusters of five, corresponding to the original five member nations in the League of Peace that founded the Hodinöhsö:ni' or Iroquoian Confederacy.

Ohskennón:ton – (Mohawk) buck or stag.

Randle Reef – (English) 630,000 cubic metres or about a million tonnes of toxic coal tar found in the 1980s underwater in Hamilton Harbour near the Stelco steel factory pier. In 1964, veteran Hamilton Harbour Commissioners marine pilot Harvey T. Randle ran aground in water that he had navigated freely for years and his name thereafter was jokingly attached to the underwater sixty-hectare toxic blob.

Roti'nikonhrakáhte – (Mohawk) in the Condolence ceremony after the people have lost a leader, this term refers to the community members whose minds are strong and upright (usually because they were not as closely related in nation or clan to the deceased).

Roti'nikonhrakwenhtará:'on – (Mohawk) in the Condolence ceremony mentioned above, refers to those whose minds have fallen flat upon the ground because of their grief.

Sakoweniónkwas – (Mohawk) traditional name of elder and traditional storyteller Tom Porter.

Scwatokwa'tshera't – (Mohawk) The Dish With One Spoon, sometimes translated as the Common Pot; refers to a particular region designated as a kind of hunting and gathering commons by surrounding Indigenous nations, where even enemies and rivals could gather food without fear of violence from other humans. Arthur Parker's summary of the Great Law of Peace lays out the principles as follows: "We shall have one dish (or bowl) in which will be placed one beaver's tail and we shall all have coequal right to it, and there shall be no knife in it, for if there be a knife in it, there would be danger that it might cut someone and blood would thereby be shed."

Shawískara – (Mohawk, sometimes spelled Tawískaron) the restless twin in the Creation Story known as Flint, who competed with Shonkwaya'tíson's creations, forming ugly, monstrous creatures instead of healthy, beautiful ones.

Shonkwaya'tíson – (Mohawk) the Creator, literally means "He has finished making our bodies."

Six Nations Confederacy Council – (English) the traditional government of the Hodninöhsö:ni' League of Six Nations, mandated in the Peacemaker's Kayaneren'tsherakowa, the Great Law of Peace. In 1924, the Canadian government forcibly removed the Confederacy Council from its Council House on the Six Nations reserve and imposed the Ottawa-based Band Council system (often referred to today as the elected council) mandated by the Indian Act. Political allegiances have been divided on the reserve ever since, between the moral authority of the traditional Confederacy Council system and the financial resources funnelled through the Ottawa-funded Band Council system.

Skadjí'nă – (Mohawk) Eagle, whose long-range vision can warn of approaching danger.

Sotsisowah – (Seneca) traditional name of professor at the University of Buffalo, now deceased, whose English name was John Mohawk.

Thaientané:ken (sometimes spelled Thayendanegea) – Joseph Brant's name in Mohawk, having two meanings: "two wagers (sticks) bound together for strength," and possibly "he who places two bets."

Tree of Peace – (English) see Onerahtase'ko:wa.

Note on pronouncing Hodinöhsö:ni' orthography:
Most of the Hodinöhsö:ni' terms used in this book are from the Mohawk language, so this note is based on Nora Deering and Helga Harries-Delisle's *Mohawk: A Teaching Grammar*

(Kahnawake: Kanien'kehaka Raotitiahkwa Cultural Centre, 1976), the textbook in the Mohawk Language class I took some years ago at McMaster University. There are other important guides and dictionaries in the Mohawk language (such as David Kanatawakhon-Maracle's *Karonon ne Owennahshonha / A Mohawk Thematic Dictionary*. London: Centre for Research and Teaching of Canadian Native Languages, University of Western Ontario, 2001), as well as among the other Hodinöhsö:ni' languages. Taylor Gibson of Deyohahá:ge: Indigenous Knowledge Centre kindly read through this Glossary and checked with language experts at Gawęnawihse' Onõda'gega' (Onondaga Language Program) on the Six Nations Reserve to ensure my approximations of Onondaga words and spellings are as accurate as possible. It is important to note that the dispersion of the Six Nations to various homelands has resulted in regional differences, so that Kahnawake Mohawk is distinct from Grand River Mohawk. In addition, the current writing system is derived from the one introduced by Jesuit French speakers in the seventeenth century, so French sensibilities have influenced spellings and accent markers. Despite these many layers, I hope the brief sketch below may help readers mouth the words that appear in this book. I should note that the English approximations below are only that: approximations for the purpose of illustration.

The colon appearing within words indicates an extended duration for the vowel sound (e.g., *fa:ther* as compared to the sound of the article *a*), while the apostrophe indicates a glottal stop blocking the passage of air, and the accent mark over a vowel indicates stress as it does in English. *En* in Mohawk is a nasal vowel that resembles the nasal in the English word *long*, while *on* is a nasal vowel that has no English equivalent. The letter *t* is pronounced *d* in Mohawk as in *door* when it appears before a vowel, otherwise it sounds like an English *t*, while the letter *k* is pronounced as a hard *g* as in *get* when it appears before a vowel. *S* is voiced when it appears before vowels like an English *z*, but otherwise unvoiced like an *s*. *S* remains unvoiced before *h* (as in *she:kon*, meaning *peace*), but becomes voiced before *i* (*si* would be *sh* in English). The cluster *ts* is pronounced *dz* as in the English word *adze*. With the above in mind, the name of Sky Woman in the Creation Story, Atsi'tsiaká:ion, would begin with the short *a* sound, stop after the first consonant cluster and then move into the extended *aahh* in the middle of the word and sound roughly like *Adzi'dzagáayoohn* in English spelling. The *r* in Mohawk is tricky for English speakers, being pronounced between an *r* and an *l*, while *ti* is pronounced like a *j*. Adding an *h* changes the sound of several consonants, so that *thi* makes an unvoiced *ch* sound, while *w*, which is usually equivalent to an English *w*, becomes *f* when an *h* is added (*wh*).

Bibliography

Anderson, A., and Grace Buttram, eds. *Other Days – Other Ways: Historical Sketches of the Binkley School District.* Hamilton, ON: printed by editors, 1965.

Arnold, Steve. "Hamilton's Average Home Price Will Hit as High as $510,000 in 2017." *Hamilton Spectator*, May 20, 2016. http://www.thespec.com/news-story/6563447-hamilton-s-average-home-price-will-hit-as-high-as-510-000-in-2017/.

Baskerville, Peter. "MacNAB, Sir ALLAN NAPIER." In *Dictionary of Canadian Biography*. Vol. 9, *1861–1870*. University of Toronto/Université Laval, 2003–. Accessed February 14, 2017. http://www.biographi.ca/en/bio/macnab_allan_napier_9E.html.

Battiste, Marie, and James (Sákéj) Youngblood Henderson. *Protecting Indigenous Knowledge and Heritage: A Global Challenge.* Saskatoon: Purich, 2000.

Beresford-Kroeger, Diana. *The Global Forest: Forty Ways Trees Can Save Us.* Toronto: Penguin, 2010.

Berry, Thomas. *The Dream of the Earth.* San Francisco: Sierra Club Books, 1988.

Berry, Wendell. "The Book of Camp Branch." In *Leavings: Poems*, 63–69. Berkeley, CA: Counterpoint, 2010.

Borson, Roo. "Snake." In *Open Wide a Wilderness: Canadian Nature Poems*, edited by Nancy Holmes, 67. Waterloo, ON: Wilfrid Laurier University Press, 2009. First published 1996.

Bouchier, Nancy B., and Ken Cruikshank. *The People and the Bay: A Social and Environmental History of Hamilton Harbour.* Vancouver: UBC Press, 2016.

"Brant Johnson." "Revolutionary War Claims for Losses: Surnames 'J.'" *Niagara Settlers*, edited by Robert Mutrie. Accessed April 26, 2016. https://sites.google.com/site/niagarasettlers/revolutionary-war -claims-j.

Brown, Dana. "Deer Hunt Puts 'People in Harm's Way.'" *Hamilton Spectator*, November 30, 2009.

Burkholder, Mabel. "The Lyons and Binkley Families of West Hamilton." *Hamilton Spectator*, December 10, 1949.

Buttrum, G.L. "The Binkley Farms." In *Ancaster's Heritage: A History of Ancaster Township.* Vol. 1, 107–8, Ancaster, ON: Ancaster Township Historical Society, 1973.

———. "The Binkley School." In *Ancaster's Heritage: A History of Ancaster Township.* Vol. 1, 108–9. Ancaster, ON: Ancaster Township Historical Society, 1973.

———. "The Binkley Union Church." In *Ancaster's Heritage: A History of Ancaster Township.* Vol. 1, 109. Ancaster, ON: Ancaster Township Historical Society, 1973.

———. "Rural Free Delivery of Mail." In *Ancaster's Heritage: A History of Ancaster Township.* Vol. 1, 109. Ancaster, ON: Ancaster Township Historical Society, 1973.

Coleman, Joey. "Randle Reef." *Hamilton Magazine*, Winter 2013. Accessed March 15, 2017.

Cooper, Tom. "Hamilton Is Having Its Moment," by Tess Kalinowski.

TheStar.com, September 3, 2016. https://www.thestar.com/business /2016/09/03/hamilton-is-having-its-moment.html.

Crawford, Gary W., and David G. Smith. "Migration in Prehistory: Princess Point and the Northern Iroquoian Case." *American Antiquity* 61, no. 4 (1996): 782–90.

Curry, Robert. *Birds of Hamilton and Surrounding Areas: Including All of Parts of Brant, Halton, Haldiman, Niagara, Norfolk, Peel, Waterloo and Wellington*. Hamilton: Hamilton Naturalists' Club, 2006.

de Lazzer, Rachel. "Poor and Dirty: In Great Lakes, Hamilton Hardest Hit by Troubling Mix of Pollution & Poverty." *Hamilton Spectator*, November 28, 2008.

Deloria, Vine, Jr. *God Is Red: A Native View of Religion*. 30th Anniversary ed. Golden, CO: Fulcrum, 2003.

Dickason, Olive, and David T. McNab. *Canada's First Nations: A History of Founding Peoples from Earliest Times*. 3rd ed. Toronto: Oxford University Press, 2002.

Drew, Benjamin. *The Refugee; or The Narratives of Fugitive Slaves in Canada. Related by Themselves, with an Account of the History and Condition of the Colored Population of Upper Canada*. Boston: John P. Jewett, 1856.

Ellul, Jacques. *The Humiliation of the Word*. Translated by Joyce Main Hanks. Grand Rapids, MI: Eerdmans, 1985. First published 1981 as *La parole humiliée* by Éditions du Seuil, 1981.

Grady, Wayne. *Toronto the Wild: Field Notes of an Urban Naturalist*. Toronto: MacFarlane, Walter, and Ross, 1995.

Green, Jeff. "Up Spencer Creek Looking for Signs of Life." *Hamilton Spectator*, August 11, 2011.

Hamilton Conservation Authority. *Ancaster Creek Subwatershed Stewardship Action Plan*, 2008. Accessed March 14, 2017. http:// conservationhamilton.ca/wp-content/uploads/sites/5/2015/07 /08May1_Ancaster_Part2_FINAL.pdf.

Daniel Coleman

———. *Sulphur Creek Subwatershed Stewardship Action Plan, 2010.* Accessed March 14, 2017. http://www.westfieldheritage.ca/images /PDFs/Planning/11_SULPHUR%20SAP.pdf.

Haskell, David George. *The Forest Unseen: A Year's Watch in Nature.* New York: Penguin, 2012.

Herring, Ann D., Heather T. Battles, Diedre Beintema, Ayla Mykytey, Thomas Siek, Katlyn Ferrusi, Brianna K. Johns, et. al. *Ch2olera: Hamilton's Forgotten Epidemics.* Hamilton: Anthropology Publications, Digital Commons@Mcmaster, 2012. Accessed March 24, 2014. http://hdl.handle.net/11375/14367.

Hill, Richard W, Sr. "The Restorative Aesthetic of Greg Staats." In *Greg Staats: Liminal Disturbance*, 3–21. Hamilton: McMaster University Museum of Art, 2011. Exhibition catalog.

———. "The Role of Deer in Haudenosaunee Culture." *Hamilton Spectator*, May 28, 2011.

Houghton, Margaret, ed. *The Hamiltonians: 100 Fascinating Lives.* Toronto: James Lorimer, 2003.

Howlett, James. "Natives and the Right to Hunt." *Hamilton Spectator,* January 5, 2011.

The Iroquois Speak Out for Mother Earth. DVD. Directed by Danny Beaton. Toronto: The Artist/Environment Forum, 2001.

Jardine, David N. *West Hamilton, a Village and a Church.* Ancaster, ON: West Hamilton Heritage Society, 1990.

Johns, Carolyn. "Non-Point Source Water Pollution Institutions in Ontario before and after Walkerton." In *Canadian Water Politics: Conflicts and Institutions*, edited by Mark Sproule-Jones, Carolyn Johns and B. Timothy Heinmiller, 203–39. Montreal: McGill-Queen's University Press, 2008.

"Johnson, Brant." "Land Petitions of The Niagara Settlers 'J.'" *Niagara Settlers*, edited by Robert Mutrie. Accessed April 26, 2016. https:// sites.google.com/site/niagarasettlers/petitions-j.

Johnson, Charles M. "A Report on the Six Nations Land Surrender of 1841." Unpublished paper.

"Johnson, Jemima, Sarah and Mary." "Land Petitions of The Niagara Settlers 'J.'" *Niagara Settlers*, edited by Robert Mutrie. Accessed April 26, 2016. https://sites.google.com/site/niagarasettlers/petitions-j.

Johnston, Basil. *Ojibway Heritage*. Toronto: McClelland & Stewart, 1976.

Kelsay, Isabel Thompson. *Joseph Brant, 1743–1807: Man of Two Worlds*. Syracuse, NY: Syracuse University Press, 1984.

Leavey, Peggy Dymond. *Molly Brant: Mohawk Loyalist and Diplomat*. Toronto: Dundurn Press, 2015.

Locke, John. "Of Property." In *Two Treatises on Government*, edited by Peter Laslett, 303–20. 2nd ed. Cambridge: Cambridge University Press, 1970.

Lyons, Oren. "Power of the Good Mind." In *New Voices from the Longhouse: An Anthology of Contemporary Iroquois Writings*, edited by Joseph Bruchac, 202–3. Greenfield Center, NY: Greenfield Review Press, 1989.

———. "Spirituality, Equality, and Natural Law." In *Pathways to Self-Determination: Canadian Indians and the Canadian State*, edited by Leroy Little Bear, Menno Boldt and J. Anthony Long, 5–21. Toronto: University of Toronto Press, 1984.

Lytwyn, Victor P. "A Dish With One Spoon: The Shared Hunting Grounds Agreement in the Great Lakes and St. Lawrence Valley Region." In *Papers of the Twenty-Eighth Algonquian Conference*, edited by David H. Pentland, 210–27. Ottawa: Carleton University, 1994.

Mackenzie, William Lyon. *Sketches of Canada and the United States*. London: Effingham Wilson, 1833.

Machado, Antonio. "I" [first poem in a section entitled "Moral Proverbs and Folk Songs"]. In *Times Alone: Selected Poems of Antonio Machado*, chosen and translated by Robert Bly, 143. Middletown, CT: Wesleyan University Press, 1983. 143.

Maracle, Brian. "The First Words." In *Our Story: Aboriginal Voices on Canada's Past*, 11–31. Toronto: Anchor Canada/The Dominion Institute, 2005.

Martin-Downs, Deborah. *One Water: Supporting Watershed Management and Green Infrastructure in Ontario Policy*. Ottawa: Ontario Water Conservation Alliance, 2010. http://www.gordonfoundation .ca/blue-economy.ca/sites/default/files/reports/resource/Ontario -Water-Conservation-Alliance-One-Water-Web.pdf.

Malcomson, Robert. "What really happened? De-bunking the Burlington Bay Sandbar Legend." *The War of 1812 Website*, 1999. Accessed September 14, 2011. http://www.warof1812.ca/burlingn.htm.

McKay, Don. "Introduction: 'Great Flint Singing.'" In *Open Wide a Wilderness: Canadian Nature Poems*, edited by Nancy Holmes, 1–32. Waterloo, ON: Wilfrid Laurier University Press, 2009.

McNeil, Mark. "Capturing the Blob at Randall's Reef." *Hamilton Spectator*, February 26, 2014.

Mohawk, John. *Iroquois Creation Story: John Arthur Gibson and J.N.B. Hewitt's Myth of the Earth Grasper*. Buffalo, NY: Mohawk Publications, 2005.

Momaday, N. Scott. "The Man Made of Words." In *Introduction to Indigenous Literary Criticism in Canada*, edited by Heather Macfarlane and Armand Garnet Ruffo, 7–19. Peterborough, ON: Broadview Press, 2015.

Morita E., Fukuda S., Nagano J., Hamajima N., Yamamoto H., Iwai Y., Nakashima T., Ohira H. and Shirakawa T. "Psychological Effects of Forest Environments on Healthy Adults: Shinrin-Yoku (Forest-Air Bathing, Walking) as a Possible Method of Stress Reduction." *Public Health* 121 no. 1 (January 2007): 54–63.

Muller, Wayne. *Sabbath: Finding Rest, Renewal, and Delight in Our Busy Lives*. New York: Bantam, 1999.

Nolan, Linda. "Out of Sight, Out of Mind? Taking Canada's Ground-water for Granted." In *Eau Canada: The Future of Canada's Water*, edited by Karen Bakker, 55–83. Vancouver: UBC Press, 2007.

Oliver, Mary. "What Can I Say." In *Swan*, 1. Boston: Beacon Press, 2010.

Ontario Invasive Plant Council. *Grow Me Instead: Beautiful Non-Invasive Plants for Your Garden*. Peterborough, ON: Ontario Invasive Plant Council, 2011.

Parker, Arthur C. *The Constitution of the Five Nations, or the Iroquois Book of the Great Law*. Ohsweken, ON: Iroqrafts, 2006. First published 1916 in *The New York Museum Bulletin*.

Pecoskie, Teri. "Deer Aren't So Dear." *Hamilton Spectator*, May 28, 2011.

The People and the Bay: The Story of Hamilton Harbour. DVD. Directed by Zack Melnick. Hamilton, ON: McMaster University/Wilson Centre for Canadian History, 2007.

Pietz, Pamela J., and Diane A. Granfors. "White-tailed deer (*Odocoileus virginianus*) Predation on Grassland Songbird Nestlings." *American Midland Naturalist* 144, no. 2 (2000): 419–22.

Porter, Tom (Sakokweniónkwas). "Creation Story Part 2" and "Creation Story Part 3." In *And Grandma Said . . . Iroquois Teachings as Passed Down Through the Oral Tradition*, 54–80. Bloomington, IN: Xlbris, 2008.

Potts, Rick. "Being Human in the Age of Humans." *National Museum of the American Indian* 14, no. 4 (Winter 2013): 27–31.

"Seneca White Deer." http://www.senecawhitedeer.org/.

———. http://en.wikipedia.org/wiki/Seneca_white_deer.

Sewatokwa'tshera't : The Dish With One Spoon. DVD. Directed by Dawn Martin-Hill. Ohsweken, ON: Haudenosaunee Confederacy, 2007.

Schindler, David. "Foreword." In *Eau Canada: The Future of Canada's Water*, edited by Karen Bakker, xi–xiv. Vancouver: UBC Press, 2007.

Daniel Coleman

Simcoe, Elizabeth. *The Diary of Mrs. John Graves Simcoe, Wife of the First Lieutenant-Governor of the Province of Upper Canada, 1792–6*, edited by J. Ross Robertson. Toronto: Prospero, 2001. First published 1911 by William Briggs.

"Sir William Johnson, 1st Baronet." Geni: A MyHeritage Company. Accessed April 26, 2016. www.geni.com/people/Sir-William -Johnson-1st-Baronet/6000000003340231324.

Six Nations Land Claims Research Office. *Outstanding Financial and Land Issues and Summary of Six Nations' Claims*. Oshweken, ON: Six Nations Lands & Resources, 1997.

Snyder, Gary. *The Practice of the Wild*. San Francisco: North Point Press, 1990.

Sproule-Jones, Mark. "Politics and Pollution on the Great Lakes: The Cleanup of Hamilton Harbour." In *Canadian Water Politics: Conflicts and Institutions*, edited by Mark Sproule-Jones, Carolyn Johns and B. Timothy Heinmiller, 179–202. Montreal: McGill-Queen's University Press, 2008.

Terpstra, John. *Falling Into Place*. Kentville, NS: Gaspereau Press, 2002.

Thomson, Thomas M. *The Spencer Story*. Hamilton: Spencer Creek Conservation Authority, 1965.

Tooker, Elisabeth. *The Iroquois Ceremonial of Midwinter*. Syracuse: Syracuse University Press, 1970.

"Traditional History of the Confederacy." In *An Anthology of Canadian Native Literature in English*. 3rd ed, edited by Daniel David Moses and Terry Goldie, 2–5. Toronto: Oxford University Press, 2005.

Waterlife: The Epic Journey of Water. DVD. Directed by Kevin McMahon. Toronto: Primitive Entertainment, 2009.

Weseloh, D.V. (Chip). "Studies of Contaminants and Population Levels of Waterbirds in Hamilton Harbour, 1970–2005." In *Birds of Hamilton and Surrounding Areas*, edited by Robert Curry, 523–41. Hamilton, ON: Hamilton Naturalists' Club, 2006.

Wong, Danielle. "Animal Traps Found in Iroquoia Heights." *Hamilton Spectator,* May 20, 2010.

———. "'Deer Pit' in Conservation Area Was Really a Kids' Fort." *Hamilton Spectator,* May 21, 2010. http://www.thespec.com/news-story/2106389--deer-pit-in-conservation-area-was-really-a-kids-fort/.

———. "Illegal Hunt Closes Mountain Conservation Area." *Hamilton Spectator,* November 12, 2009. http://www.thespec.com/news-story/2089361-illegal-hunt-closes-mountain-conservation-area/.

———. "Treaty Covers HCA Lands: Bentley." *Hamilton Spectator,* June 6, 2011. http://www.thespec.com/news-story/2206545-treaty-covers-hca-lands-bentley/.

Woodhouse, T. Roy. "The Binkleys of Binkley Hollow." In *Ancaster's Heritage: A History of Ancaster Township.* Vol. 1, 106–7. Ancaster, ON: Ancaster Township Historical Society, 1973.

Daniel Coleman was born and raised the child of Canadian missionary parents in Ethiopia, an experience he has written about in *The Scent of Eucalyptus: A Missionary Childhood in Ethiopia*. He moved to the Canadian prairies in the 1980s and completed his PhD in Canadian Literature at the University of Alberta in 1995. He went on to publish scholarly books on Canadian immigrant writing and on how Canada became a white, British place. Since 1997, he has lived in Hamilton, Ontario, where he teaches Canadian Literature at McMaster University.